THE MOST AMAZING STORIES IN Sports FOR KIDS

20 Inspirational Stories That Defined Sports

Jordan Chase

Table Of Contents

Introduction.....................1
The Miracle on Ice.....................3
Wayne Gretzky's Record-Breaking Journey.....................10
Jackie Robinson Breaks the Color Barrier.....................16
Kirk Gibson's Legendary Home Run.....................23
Cal Ripken Jr.'s Iron Man Streak.....................29
Michael Jordan's "Flu Game".....................35
The Birth of March Madness: NC State's Miracle Run.....................41
LeBron James: The Kid from Akron.....................47
The Ice Bowl: Packers vs. Cowboys.....................53
Tom Brady: The Comeback King.....................59
Walter Payton's Heart of a Champion.....................66
The Hand of God and the Goal of the Century.....................72
The U.S. Women's National Team Wins the 1999 World Cup.....................78
Lionel Messi's First World Cup Win.....................84
Bo Jackson: The Greatest Two-Sport Athlete.....................90
Simone Biles: The Queen of Gymnastics.....................96
Usain Bolt: The Lightning Bolt's Record-Breaking Speed.....................102
The Miracle at Augusta: Tiger Woods' 2019 Masters Comeback.....................108
Muhammad Ali: The Rumble in the Jungle.....................114
Michael Phelps: The Greatest Olympian of All Time.....................120
Conclusion.....................126

Welcome to The Most Amazing Moments in Sports For Kids!

Sports are more than just games—they're stories of courage, determination, and heart. They show us what's possible when we work hard, believe in ourselves, and never give up. This book is a collection of some of the most inspiring sports stories ever told—moments when athletes didn't just win, but overcame incredible odds to achieve greatness.

You'll read about Muhammad Ali's legendary fight, Simone Biles redefining gymnastics, and Michael Phelps breaking records in the pool. These athletes faced challenges, failures, and doubts, yet they persevered, proving that true champions are made through resilience and hard work.

This book is for anyone who dreams big—whether it's scoring the winning goal, achieving a personal best, or simply becoming the best version of yourself. These stories will inspire you to chase your dreams, no matter how big they are.

Your journey starts here. Let's dive in.

The Miracle on Ice

How an Underdog Team Changed the World of Hockey

In the winter of 1980, the sleepy town of Lake Placid, New York, became the center of the sports universe. Snow blanketed the landscape, the air was cold and crisp, and the world had gathered for the Winter Olympics. But in the midst of all the events taking place, one hockey game stood out above all others. It wasn't just a game; it became a defining moment in sports history and a symbol of hope for millions of people. This is the story of the "Miracle on Ice," a tale of courage, teamwork, and the belief that anything is possible.

The year was 1980, and the Cold War between the United States and the Soviet Union was at its peak. The world seemed divided, with these two superpowers constantly competing—not just in politics or space exploration, but in sports as well. For years, the Soviet Union's hockey team had been a dominant force. They had won gold medals in the last four Winter Olympics, and their players were considered the best in the world. Their team was a well-oiled machine, composed of athletes who trained together year-round. They were so good that many people believed they couldn't be beaten.

On the other side of the rink was the United States hockey team, a group of young college players with little experience in international competition. They were not professionals like the Soviets, and most of them had never played a game at this level. The Americans were underdogs in every sense of the word. Few believed they could win, and even fewer thought they stood a chance against the mighty Soviet team.

The story began months before the Olympics, when Herb Brooks, a former hockey player turned coach, was tasked with assembling the U.S. team. Herb was known for his fiery personality and his innovative coaching methods. He wasn't interested in picking the best individual players; instead, he wanted to build a team that could work together as one. He scouted players from colleges across the country, looking for athletes who had skill, determination, and the willingness to put the team above themselves.

When Herb announced his final roster, many people were surprised. He left out some of the biggest names in college hockey and instead chose players who were willing to embrace his vision. But there was a problem: many of these players were rivals. They came from different colleges and had spent years competing against each other. Herb knew this, and he also knew that if they didn't learn to work together, they would never stand a chance against the Soviets.

Training began in the summer of 1979, and it was grueling. Herb pushed the players harder than they had ever been pushed before. His practices were intense, his drills were relentless, and his expectations were sky-high. He demanded not just physical toughness but also mental toughness. One of his most famous sayings was, "You don't have enough talent to win on talent alone." He drilled this idea into the team every day, reminding them that success would come from hard work, discipline, and unity.

The team's first test came in a series of exhibition games leading up to the Olympics. They played teams from other countries, and the results were mixed. Sometimes they won, sometimes they lost, but Herb was more focused on how the team was coming together. He wanted them to trust each other, to play for the name on the front of their jerseys—"USA"—rather than the name on the back.

One of the most pivotal moments in their preparation came after a disappointing performance in an exhibition game against Norway. The players had been sloppy, and Herb was furious. After the game, instead of letting them leave the rink, he made them stay and skate sprints. Over and over again, he blew his whistle, yelling, "Again!" The players were exhausted, their legs felt like jelly, and some of them could barely stand. But Herb didn't stop. He wanted them to understand that wearing the USA jersey meant something. It wasn't just about hockey; it was about representing their country.

By the time the Olympics began in February 1980, the U.S. team was ready. They were still considered underdogs, but they had something special: they believed in each other. Their first few games went better than expected. They tied Sweden in their opening match and then defeated Czechoslovakia, a team that was ranked as one of the best in the world. With each game, their confidence grew, and the nation began to take notice.

Then came February 22, the day they would face the Soviet Union in the semifinal round. The Soviets had been dominating their competition, as everyone expected. They had crushed teams like Japan and Poland, scoring goal after goal with ease. Most people believed that the U.S. team would be no different, that they would be just another victim of the Soviet machine. But Herb and his players had other plans.

The game began in front of a packed arena in Lake Placid. The energy in the building was electric, with fans waving American flags and chanting "U-S-A!" From the very start, the Soviets showed why they were considered the best. Their passing was precise, their skating was flawless, and their shots were powerful. They scored the first goal early in the game, and it looked like it was going to be a long night for the Americans.

But the U.S. team didn't back down. They fought hard, blocking shots, making plays, and giving everything they had. By the end of the first period, the score was tied 2-2. The crowd erupted with excitement, realizing that the Americans were not going to be an easy opponent.

In the second period, the Soviets regained control. Their skill and experience were on full display, and they scored another goal to take the lead. But the Americans held their ground, refusing to let the game slip away. They played with heart, determination, and a level of grit that surprised even their coach.

As the third period began, the score was 3-2 in favor of the Soviets. The Americans knew they had to dig deep if they wanted to have a chance. Then, with just ten minutes left in the game, something incredible happened. Mike Eruzione, the team captain, found himself with the puck in front of the Soviet net. He took a shot, and it sailed past the goalie into the back of the net. The crowd erupted as the Americans tied the game 3-3.

Minutes later, the unthinkable happened. Another American player, Mark Johnson, scored again, giving the U.S. team a 4-3 lead. The arena was deafening, with fans cheering and chanting louder than ever. But there were still several minutes left on the clock, and the Soviets were not going to go down without a fight.

The final minutes of the game were some of the most intense in hockey history. The Soviets attacked relentlessly, firing shot after shot at the American goalie, Jim Craig. But Jim stood tall, making save after save, deflecting pucks with his pads, stick, and gloves. The clock ticked down, and the tension in the arena was unbearable.

"Ten seconds left... You've got five seconds left in the game. Do you believe in miracles? Yes!" shouted the announcer as the final buzzer sounded. The Americans had done it. They had beaten the seemingly unbeatable Soviet team.

The players threw their gloves in the air and hugged each other, tears streaming down their faces. The crowd was in a frenzy, chanting and celebrating one of the greatest upsets in sports history. The victory wasn't just about hockey; it was about hope, determination, and the belief that anything is possible.

Two days later, the U.S. team defeated Finland to win the gold medal. But it was their victory over the Soviets that became a defining moment in sports history. It was more than just a game; it was a story of courage, unity, and the power of believing in yourself.

"Great moments are born from great opportunities."
— **Herb Brooks**

Wayne Gretzky's Record-Breaking Journey

How "The Great One" Changed Hockey Forever

The game of hockey has seen countless incredible players. But when it comes to sheer dominance, skill, and impact on the sport, one name stands above all others: Wayne Gretzky. Known as "The Great One,"

Wayne Gretzky didn't just play hockey—he redefined it. This is the story of how a skinny kid from a small Canadian town became the greatest hockey player the world has ever known.

Wayne Gretzky was born on January 26, 1961, in Brantford, Ontario, Canada. From the very beginning, it was clear that Wayne was special. His parents, Walter and Phyllis Gretzky, noticed how much Wayne loved hockey, even as a toddler. By the time he was two years old, he was already skating. Walter, who loved hockey himself, built a rink in the family's backyard. It wasn't big or fancy, but it became Wayne's favorite place in the world.

Wayne spent countless hours on that backyard rink, practicing his skating, shooting, and stickhandling. He wasn't the fastest skater or the strongest player, but Wayne had something that set him apart: his mind. Even as a kid, Wayne saw the game differently. He had an almost magical ability to anticipate what would happen next. While other players followed the puck, Wayne went where the puck was going to be.

By the time Wayne was six, he was playing hockey with kids much older than him. It wasn't uncommon for him to play with boys who were ten or eleven years old—and dominate. Coaches and parents couldn't believe how skilled he was. He could pass the puck perfectly, score goals with ease, and make plays that seemed impossible for someone so young.

As Wayne got older, his legend grew. When he was ten years old, he scored an astonishing 378 goals in a single season while playing for the Brantford Nadrofsky Steelers. That's right—378 goals in just one season! His incredible performance drew national attention, and soon, everyone in Canada was talking about the kid from Brantford who seemed destined for greatness.

But Wayne's journey wasn't always easy. Because he was so good, some parents and players became jealous. They accused him of being too old to play with younger kids or claimed he was getting special treatment. Wayne didn't let the negativity bother him. Instead, he focused on what he loved most: playing hockey. His father, Walter, always reminded him to stay humble, work hard, and let his actions on the ice speak for themselves.

When Wayne turned 14, he left home to play junior hockey in Toronto, a big step for a young boy. It was difficult for Wayne to leave his family, but he knew it was necessary to achieve his dream of playing professional hockey. In Toronto, Wayne continued to dominate, but now he was facing older, bigger, and stronger players. Despite the challenges, he thrived, proving that his talent and determination could overcome any obstacle.

At 17, Wayne joined the World Hockey Association (WHA), signing with the Indianapolis Racers. But his time there was short-lived. The team traded him to the Edmonton Oilers, where his career truly began to take off. When the WHA merged with the NHL in 1979, Wayne and the Oilers joined the league. It didn't take long for Wayne to make his mark.

In his first NHL season, Wayne scored an incredible 137 points, tying for the league lead in scoring. He was named the NHL's Most Valuable Player (MVP), an award he would go on to win eight years in a row—a record that still stands today. But Wayne wasn't just about individual accomplishments. He was a team player who made everyone around him better. His passing was so precise and unselfish that teammates often joked he had eyes in the back of his head.

Over the next decade, Wayne shattered nearly every scoring record in hockey. He scored 50 goals in just 39 games during the 1981-82 season, a feat that has never been matched. He became the only player in NHL history to score more than 200 points in a single season—a mark he achieved not once, but four times. Wayne's vision, creativity, and hockey IQ were unmatched. Defenders couldn't stop him, goalies couldn't outsmart him, and fans couldn't get enough of him.

Wayne's success wasn't limited to the regular season. He led the Edmonton Oilers to four Stanley Cup championships in the 1980s, cementing his legacy as one of the greatest players in team sports history. His ability to perform under pressure and deliver in clutch moments made him a fan favorite and a nightmare for opponents.

But Wayne's journey wasn't just about breaking records and winning championships. He carried himself with humility and grace, always crediting his teammates and coaches for his success. He never bragged or acted like he was better than anyone else, even though his achievements made it clear that he was. Wayne understood that hockey was a team sport and that no one, not even "The Great One," could succeed alone.

In 1988, Wayne was traded to the Los Angeles Kings, a move that shocked the hockey world. Many fans in Edmonton were heartbroken to see their hero leave, but Wayne embraced the challenge of bringing hockey to a new market. In Los Angeles, he helped popularize the sport in the United States, inspiring a new generation of fans and players. His influence extended far beyond the rink, as he became a global ambassador for hockey and a role model for millions.

Wayne Gretzky retired in 1999, leaving the game as the most accomplished player in NHL history. By the time he hung up his skates, he held more than 60 NHL records, including the most goals (894), assists (1,963), and points (2,857). Many of his records are considered unbreakable, and his impact on the sport is immeasurable.

Wayne's story is one of talent, hard work, and unwavering determination. He wasn't the biggest or the strongest player, but he used his intelligence, creativity, and love for the game to achieve greatness. He showed the world that with passion and perseverance, anything is possible.

Even after retirement, Wayne continued to inspire. He coached, mentored young players, and remained involved in the hockey community. His legacy lives on, not just in the record books, but in the hearts of everyone who loves the game.

"You miss 100% of the shots you don't take."
— **Wayne Gretzky**

Jackie Robinson Breaks the Color Barrier

How One Man Changed Baseball and America Forever

In the spring of 1947, under a bright Brooklyn sun, a young African American man named Jackie Robinson stepped onto the field at Ebbets Field. The crowd roared—not with cheers, but with taunts and jeers. Wearing the number 42 on his back, Jackie wasn't just playing a game of baseball; he was making history. Jackie Robinson was about to break Major League Baseball's color barrier, becoming the first Black player in a sport that had been segregated for over half a century. His journey to that moment was filled with trials, triumphs, and extraordinary courage, and it would forever change the landscape of sports and society.

Jack Roosevelt Robinson was born on January 31, 1919, in Cairo, Georgia, to a family of sharecroppers. He was the youngest of five siblings, raised by his mother, Mallie Robinson, after his father left when Jackie was just a baby. Mallie moved the family to Pasadena, California, in search of better opportunities, but life was anything but easy. They lived in a predominantly white neighborhood, where they faced racism and hostility. Mallie, however, was a woman of immense strength and resilience. She instilled in Jackie and his siblings the values of hard work, dignity, and self-respect, teaching them to stand up for what was right and never let anyone make them feel inferior.

From an early age, Jackie showed an extraordinary talent for sports. He excelled at nearly every game he played, whether it was basketball, football, track, or tennis. But it was his determination and competitive spirit that truly set him apart. He hated losing and would work tirelessly to improve his skills. Jackie attended John Muir High School, where his athletic abilities became impossible to ignore. He was the star of the football team, the basketball team, the track team, and, of course, the baseball team. Even at this young age, Jackie's potential was clear to everyone who watched him play.

After high school, Jackie went to Pasadena Junior College, where he continued to shine as a multi-sport athlete. His performances on the field and track caught the attention of scouts, and he was soon offered a scholarship to UCLA. There, Jackie achieved something no other athlete at the university had done: he lettered in four sports—football, basketball, track, and baseball. While baseball would eventually become his claim to fame, it was actually his weakest sport in college. Still, Jackie's all-around athleticism was undeniable.

Yet despite his success, Jackie faced constant challenges because of his race. He was often the only Black player on his teams, and he encountered racism from fans, opponents, and even teammates. Hotels and restaurants frequently refused to serve him when the team traveled. Instead of letting these injustices crush his spirit, Jackie used them as fuel to push himself harder. His ability to stay focused in the face of adversity would become one of his greatest strengths.

In 1941, just before graduating, Jackie left UCLA to help support his family. He took a job as an athletic director for a youth program and later joined the U.S. Army during World War II. It was during his time in the military that Jackie's sense of justice and courage truly came to the forefront. In 1944, while stationed in Texas, Jackie was court-martialed for refusing to move to the back of a segregated bus. This act of defiance foreshadowed the strength and determination he would later display in breaking baseball's color barrier. Although he was eventually acquitted, the experience solidified his commitment to fighting injustice wherever he encountered it.

After being honorably discharged from the Army, Jackie returned to his first love: baseball. In 1945, he joined the Kansas City Monarchs, a team in the Negro Leagues. At the time, Major League Baseball was still segregated, and Black players were not allowed to compete with white players. The Negro Leagues provided an opportunity for African American athletes to showcase their incredible talent, but the conditions were far from ideal. The players often had to endure long bus rides, poor facilities, and low pay. Despite these challenges, Jackie's performance on the field was outstanding. He batted .387 that season and quickly became one of the league's brightest stars.

Jackie's talent didn't go unnoticed. That same year, Branch Rickey, the general manager of the Brooklyn Dodgers, decided it was time to integrate Major League Baseball. Rickey believed that segregation in baseball was not only unfair but also harmful to the sport. He began searching for the right player to break the color barrier. Rickey wasn't just looking for a great athlete; he needed someone with extraordinary courage, character, and self-control. The player would have to endure relentless racism and hostility without fighting back.

When Rickey met Jackie, he knew he had found his man. During their first meeting, Rickey warned Jackie about the challenges he would face if he joined the Dodgers. He would be called names, spat on, and even threatened. "I'm looking for a player with guts enough not to fight back," Rickey said. Jackie thought for a moment and then responded, "Do you want a player who doesn't have the guts to fight back?" Rickey smiled. "No, I want a player who has the guts not to fight back." Jackie understood what was being asked of him, and he agreed to take on the challenge.

In 1946, Jackie signed a contract with the Dodgers and was assigned to their minor league affiliate, the Montreal Royals. That season, Jackie faced constant discrimination from fans, opponents, and even some of his own teammates. But he also experienced moments of kindness and support. The people of Montreal embraced him, and his performance on the field was nothing short of spectacular. Jackie led the league in batting average and quickly became a fan favorite.

On April 15, 1947, Jackie Robinson made his debut with the Brooklyn Dodgers. It was a day that would go down in history. The reaction to Jackie's presence in the Major Leagues was immediate and intense. While many fans and players admired his courage, others were openly hostile. Opposing pitchers threw at his head, baserunners tried to spike him with their cleats, and fans shouted racial slurs from the stands. Some of his own teammates initially refused to play with him.

Through it all, Jackie remained composed. He knew that if he retaliated, it would give his detractors an excuse to call the integration experiment a failure. Instead, he let his performance on the field do the talking. Jackie's speed, power, and intelligence made him one of the most exciting players in the league. He stole bases with ease, hit for average and power, and played stellar defense. By the end of his rookie season, Jackie had won the National League Rookie of the Year award, cementing his place as one of baseball's brightest stars.

Jackie's impact went far beyond his stats. He became a symbol of hope and inspiration for millions of African Americans who saw him as proof that barriers could be broken. His courage in the face of adversity showed the world that racism had no place in sports—or society. Over the next decade, Jackie continued to excel. He was a six-time All-Star, won the National League MVP award in 1949, and helped lead the Dodgers to six National League pennants and one World Series championship in 1955.

After retiring from baseball in 1957, Jackie remained a tireless advocate for civil rights and social justice. He used his fame to speak out against inequality and worked to create opportunities for African Americans in business, politics, and education. Jackie's efforts extended far beyond the baseball diamond; he believed that his role as a trailblazer came with the responsibility to make the world a better place.

Jackie Robinson passed away in 1972, but his legacy lives on. In 1997, Major League Baseball retired his number, 42, across all teams, ensuring that no player would ever wear it again. Every year on April 15, players and coaches throughout the league wear the number 42 in his honor. Jackie's story is a testament to the power of courage, perseverance, and the belief that one person can make a difference.

"A life is not important except in the impact it has on other lives."

— Jackie Robinson

Kirk Gibson's Legendary Home Run

How One Swing of the Bat Defined Perseverance and Determination

Baseball has long been a game of unforgettable moments. Home runs that soar into the night, jaw-dropping catches, and game-saving pitches have etched themselves into the minds of fans. But few moments in the sport's history carry the emotional weight, drama, and sheer improbability of Kirk Gibson's legendary home run in Game 1 of the 1988 World Series. It wasn't just a home run—it was a testament to perseverance, determination, and the idea that greatness can be achieved even in the face of insurmountable odds.

The 1988 Los Angeles Dodgers entered the postseason as underdogs. Their roster was filled with talented but unheralded players, and their season had been marked by injuries and inconsistency. Despite the challenges, the Dodgers managed to claw their way to the World Series to face the heavily favored Oakland Athletics. The Athletics were a powerhouse team, led by the dynamic duo of Jose Canseco and Mark McGwire, known as the "Bash Brothers." With their explosive offense and dominant pitching, the Athletics seemed destined to steamroll the Dodgers and claim the championship.

Among the Dodgers' key players was Kirk Gibson, a gritty and determined outfielder whose fierce competitive spirit had been a driving force all season. Gibson had joined the Dodgers earlier that year and quickly established himself as a leader. He wasn't just a skilled player; he was a fighter who inspired his teammates with his passion and refusal to quit. But as the World Series began, Gibson's season appeared to be over. He was battling injuries to both legs—a strained left hamstring and a swollen right knee—that left him barely able to walk, let alone run or swing a bat.

As Game 1 unfolded on October 15, 1988, at Dodger Stadium, the Athletics wasted no time showing their dominance. In the first inning, Jose Canseco crushed a grand slam, giving the Athletics a commanding 4-2 lead. The Dodgers managed to chip away at the deficit, but as the game entered the bottom of the ninth inning, they still trailed 4-3. The atmosphere was tense, and the crowd of 55,000 fans seemed resigned to a disappointing loss.

Meanwhile, Kirk Gibson sat in the Dodgers' clubhouse, watching the game unfold on a small television. He hadn't suited up for the game, convinced that his injuries would keep him off the field. But as the innings passed and the stakes grew higher, Gibson's competitive fire began to burn. He listened to the cheers of the crowd, watched his teammates fight to stay in the game, and felt the weight of the moment. Slowly, painfully, he began testing his swing in the clubhouse. Each motion sent waves of pain through his body, but Gibson pushed through it, telling himself he might still have something to offer.

As the bottom of the ninth inning began, the Dodgers' hopes rested on a slim thread. With one out and the tying run on first base, Dodgers manager Tommy Lasorda decided to take a chance. He turned to his bench and called on Kirk Gibson. The decision shocked everyone. How could a player so injured, who hadn't even warmed up, possibly face

Dennis Eckersley, the Athletics' star closer and one of the best pitchers in baseball?

Gibson emerged from the dugout to a roar of disbelief and excitement from the crowd. He hobbled to the plate, his body visibly stiff and unsteady. The announcers couldn't believe what they were seeing. "Gibson will pinch-hit," one of them said, incredulously. "And with two bad legs, he's trying to win the game with one swing."

The odds were stacked against Gibson in every way. Eckersley was at the top of his game, known for his devastating slider and pinpoint control. Gibson, on the other hand, hadn't faced live pitching in days and was in excruciating pain. But none of that mattered to Gibson. He had come too far to back down now.

The first pitch was a ball. Gibson stepped out of the batter's box, adjusting his stance and grimacing in pain. The second pitch was a strike, a sharp slider that cut across the plate. Gibson fouled off the next two pitches, barely keeping himself in the at-bat. Each swing seemed to take every ounce of strength he had. He was visibly struggling, leaning on his bat for support between pitches.

Then, Gibson remembered something. One of his teammates had told him about Eckersley's habit of throwing a backdoor slider—a pitch that looked like it was going outside the strike zone but curved back in at the last second. If he could anticipate that pitch, he might have a chance.

With the count at 3-2, Eckersley prepared to deliver the next pitch. The crowd was on its feet, holding its collective breath. Gibson dug in, focusing all his energy on what might be his final swing of the season. Eckersley wound up and released the ball. Gibson saw the pitch, recognized the slider, and swung with everything he had.

The crack of the bat meeting the ball echoed through the stadium. The ball soared high into the night sky, carrying deep into right field. For a moment, time seemed to stand still. Fans, players, and announcers alike watched in awe as the ball sailed over the fence and into the stands.

Gibson had done it. A two-run, walk-off home run to win the game for the Dodgers. The crowd erupted into a deafening roar, the kind of cheer that shakes the ground and echoes in memory. Gibson began his slow, painful journey around the bases, pumping his fist in the air as he rounded first base—a gesture that would become one of the most iconic images in baseball history.

When Gibson finally reached home plate, he was mobbed by his teammates, who lifted him into the air in celebration. The Dodgers had pulled off an improbable victory, and Gibson had delivered one of the most dramatic moments in sports history.

The impact of Gibson's home run went far beyond Game 1. It set the tone for the rest of the series, inspiring the Dodgers and demoralizing the Athletics. The Dodgers, riding the momentum of that magical moment, went on to win the World Series in five games. Gibson's heroics became a symbol of resilience and determination, a reminder that anything is possible with the right mindset.

Years later, Gibson reflected on that night and what it meant to him. He admitted that he hadn't been sure he could do it, but he knew he had to try. "You have to believe in yourself," he said. "Even when the odds are against you, even when it feels impossible, you have to believe you can make a difference."

Kirk Gibson's legendary home run remains one of the most cherished moments in baseball history. It's a story that reminds us that greatness isn't about being perfect—it's about rising to the occasion, no matter the challenges.

"A hero is someone who, in spite of weakness, doubt, or not always knowing the answers, goes ahead and overcomes anyway."

— Kirk Gibson

Cal Ripken Jr.'s Iron Man Streak

How One Player's Commitment Changed the Game of Baseball Forever

On the evening of September 6, 1995, the Baltimore Orioles' Camden Yards was packed with fans. The stadium was buzzing with excitement, not because of a close playoff race or a thrilling matchup, but because history was about to be made. Cal Ripken Jr., the Orioles' beloved shortstop, was about to play in his 2,131st consecutive Major League Baseball game, breaking the record set by the legendary Lou Gehrig over half a century earlier. This wasn't just a game; it was a celebration of dedication, perseverance, and love for baseball. It marked the culmination of a journey that inspired millions and solidified Ripken's place as one of the greatest players in baseball history.

Calvin Edwin Ripken Jr. was born on August 24, 1960, in Havre de Grace, Maryland. From the very beginning, baseball was in his blood. His father, Cal Ripken Sr., was a baseball lifer—a player, coach, and manager in the Baltimore Orioles organization. The Ripken family lived and breathed baseball, and young Cal grew up on the game. He spent countless hours at the ballpark, watching his father work and dreaming of one day playing in the Major Leagues himself.

Despite his natural talent, Cal wasn't a flashy player. He wasn't the fastest runner, the strongest hitter, or the most agile fielder. But what he lacked in raw athleticism, he made up for with an unparalleled work ethic and an unwavering commitment to the game. Cal believed that success wasn't about being the most gifted; it was about showing up every day, working hard, and doing your best no matter what.

Cal's journey to the Major Leagues began in the Orioles' minor league system, where he honed his skills and proved his worth. He was drafted by the Orioles in 1978 and made his Major League debut on August 10,

1981. The following season, Ripken became the Orioles' starting shortstop, a position he would hold for much of his career. From the moment he stepped onto the field, it was clear that Cal was something special.

In 1982, Cal Ripken Jr. played in every single game of the season, a rarity in a sport where injuries, fatigue, and slumps often force players to take days off. That year, he won the American League Rookie of the Year award, an impressive feat for a young player still finding his footing in the big leagues. But Ripken wasn't satisfied with just being good—he wanted to be great.

Cal quickly earned a reputation as one of the most dependable players in baseball. He wasn't just reliable; he was exceptional. In 1983, he won the American League MVP award and led the Orioles to a World Series championship, their first since 1970. Fans admired his consistent performance, his quiet leadership, and his ability to deliver in clutch moments. But what truly set Cal apart was his incredible durability.

Baseball is a demanding sport. Teams play 162 games a season, often with little rest between games. The grind of travel, practice, and competition takes a toll on even the toughest players. Most players, even the best, need occasional days off to recover. But not Cal Ripken Jr. From the moment he became the Orioles' starting shortstop, Cal played every single game, no matter what.

His streak began on May 30, 1982, and it quickly became the stuff of legend. Year after year, Cal showed up to the ballpark, ready to play. He battled through minor injuries, sickness, and personal challenges, refusing to let anything keep him off the field. His dedication was a testament to his love for the game and his commitment to his team.

There were times when continuing the streak wasn't easy. In 1985, Cal suffered a severe ankle injury during a game. Most players would have taken time off to heal, but not Cal. He taped up his ankle, gritted his teeth, and kept playing. His determination inspired his teammates and earned the respect of fans and opponents alike.

By the early 1990s, Cal's streak was approaching Lou Gehrig's record of 2,130 consecutive games played. Gehrig, known as the "Iron Horse," had set the record in 1939, and many believed it would never be broken. But as Cal's streak continued to grow, fans began to believe that he could achieve the impossible.

The buildup to September 6, 1995, was electric. Baseball had endured a difficult period the previous year, with a players' strike that canceled the 1994 World Series and left many fans disillusioned. Cal's pursuit of Gehrig's record became a beacon of hope, a reminder of everything that was good about the game. Fans flocked to ballparks to witness history in the making, and the media coverage was relentless.

When the historic night finally arrived, the atmosphere at Camden Yards was unlike anything the sport had ever seen. The Orioles were playing the California Angels, but the outcome of the game seemed almost secondary. Everyone was there to celebrate Cal Ripken Jr.

As the game began, the anticipation was palpable. Fans cheered wildly every time Cal stepped onto the field or came up to bat. In the fifth inning, Cal hit a home run, sending the crowd into a frenzy. It was a perfect moment, a fitting tribute to his extraordinary career.

Then, in the middle of the fifth inning, the game became official, and Cal Ripken Jr. was officially the new Iron Man of baseball. The stadium erupted in applause, and the game came to a halt as players, coaches, and fans honored Cal's achievement. A banner was unfurled in center field, reading "2,131," and Cal took a victory lap around the stadium, high-fiving fans and soaking in the moment.

The celebration lasted over 20 minutes, but it wasn't just about breaking a record. It was about what the record represented: dedication, perseverance, and an unwavering commitment to excellence. Cal's streak reminded everyone that greatness isn't just about talent; it's about showing up every day, giving your best, and never giving up.

Cal Ripken Jr. went on to extend his streak to 2,632 consecutive games before voluntarily ending it on September 20, 1998. He believed that the time had come to step aside and give others a chance to play. By the time he retired in 2001, Cal had cemented his legacy as one of the greatest players in baseball history. He was inducted into the Baseball Hall of Fame in 2007, receiving one of the highest voting percentages in history.

Today, Cal Ripken Jr.'s Iron Man streak remains one of the most iconic achievements in sports. It's a story that transcends baseball, inspiring people of all ages and backgrounds to strive for greatness in their own lives.

"You can't get much done in life if you only work on the days you feel good."

— **Cal Ripken Jr.**

Michael Jordan's "Flu Game"

How a Legend Rose Above the Odds in His Most Iconic Performance

It was June 11, 1997, and the Delta Center in Salt Lake City, Utah, was packed with fans eager to see Game 5 of the NBA Finals. The Chicago Bulls, led by Michael Jordan, were facing off against the Utah Jazz, with the series tied at two games apiece. For basketball fans, this was a pivotal moment. The stakes couldn't have been higher. The winner of Game 5 would take a commanding lead in the best-of-seven series, inching closer to the championship. But as the game approached, whispers began to circulate: something was wrong with Michael Jordan.

That day, Jordan wasn't his usual unstoppable self. Known for his incredible athleticism, laser-sharp focus, and fierce competitiveness, Jordan had a reputation for stepping up when the stakes were highest. But on this day, something was different. Fans who saw him warming up noticed he seemed sluggish. His movements were slower, and his usually intense gaze lacked its usual fire. The truth soon emerged—Michael Jordan was sick.

Jordan had woken up in the middle of the night with severe chills, sweating profusely, and barely able to get out of bed. The team's medical staff quickly determined that he was suffering from flu-like symptoms, possibly food poisoning. He had a high fever, dehydration, and nausea. His energy was gone, and just walking felt like a monumental task. For any other player, stepping onto the court in such a condition would have been unthinkable. But Michael Jordan wasn't any other player.

From the moment he entered the league in 1984, Jordan had established himself as one of the greatest basketball players of all time. His combination of skill, athleticism, and mental toughness set him apart from his peers. He wasn't just a player; he was a force of nature, capable of dominating games and inspiring his teammates to rise to his level. Jordan lived for moments like the NBA Finals, where legends were made and championships won.

As Game 5 approached, Jordan knew the stakes. The Jazz were a formidable team, led by Karl Malone and John Stockton, two of the greatest players in NBA history. The Bulls had battled hard to split the first four games, and with the series tied, Game 5 was crucial. A loss would put the Bulls in a dangerous position, needing to win two straight games to secure the title. Jordan knew his team needed him, and despite his illness, he was determined to play.

When the game began, it was clear that Jordan was far from 100%. He moved slowly, his face pale and drenched with sweat. Each step seemed to take tremendous effort, and his usually sharp shooting was off. The Jazz took advantage, racing to an early lead as their home crowd roared in approval. For a moment, it seemed like the Bulls were in trouble.

But then, something remarkable happened. As the first quarter wore on, Jordan began to find his rhythm. He hit a jumper, then another. Slowly, the energy that had seemed absent began to return. By the second quarter, he was taking over the game in the way only Michael Jordan could. Despite his condition, he scored from all over the court, attacking the basket, sinking jump shots, and drawing fouls.

Jordan's performance wasn't just about scoring—it was about willpower. Every movement, every play, seemed to defy the limits of the human body. His teammates, inspired by his determination, stepped up their game. Scottie Pippen, Jordan's trusted teammate and friend, helped carry the load, setting up plays and providing crucial support. But even with Pippen's help, the Bulls were in a dogfight.

The Jazz weren't going down without a fight. Karl Malone, the league's MVP that season, was dominant in the paint, using his strength and skill to score at will. John Stockton orchestrated the offense with precision, finding open teammates and hitting key shots. The Jazz fed off their home crowd's energy, and by halftime, the game was still close.

In the locker room during halftime, Jordan collapsed into a chair, barely able to keep his eyes open. The team's medical staff urged him to rest, to consider sitting out the second half. But Jordan shook his head. "I'm playing," he said, his voice weak but firm.

As the second half began, Jordan continued his heroic effort. Every play seemed to drain him, yet he kept going. He hit contested jump shots, drove to the basket, and even played solid defense. His intensity never wavered, even as his body threatened to give out. The Bulls and Jazz traded leads throughout the second half, with neither team able to pull away.

By the fourth quarter, the game had reached a fever pitch. The Jazz clung to a narrow lead, and the Bulls desperately needed a spark. That spark, as always, came from Michael Jordan. With just minutes remaining, Jordan hit a crucial three-pointer, giving the Bulls a lead they would never relinquish. The shot was pure determination—a testament to Jordan's refusal to let his illness define him.

As the final seconds ticked away, the Bulls secured a hard-fought 90-88 victory. Jordan had scored an astonishing 38 points, along with seven rebounds, five assists, three steals, and one block. When the buzzer sounded, Jordan collapsed into Scottie Pippen's arms, utterly exhausted. It was a moment of raw emotion, a symbol of what it had taken for him to deliver such a performance.

The Bulls went on to win the series in Game 6, capturing their fifth championship of the decade. But it was Game 5—forever known as "The Flu Game"—that cemented Jordan's legacy as the ultimate competitor.

Jordan's performance that night wasn't just about basketball. It was about grit, resilience, and the power of the human spirit. It showed the world that greatness isn't about being perfect or invincible—it's about rising to the occasion, even when everything seems stacked against you.

Years later, Jordan reflected on that night, saying, "I didn't have the energy to think about what I couldn't do. I just focused on what I could do." His words captured the essence of his greatness—the ability to push beyond limits and find a way to succeed, no matter the circumstances.

Michael Jordan's "Flu Game" remains one of the most iconic moments in sports history. It's a story that inspires athletes and fans alike, a reminder that true greatness comes from within.

"Sometimes, you have to play with your heart when your body has nothing left."

— Michael Jordan

The Birth of March Madness: NC State's Miracle Run

How an Underdog Team Captured the Hearts of a Nation

Every March, basketball fans across the United States gather around their televisions, filling out brackets and cheering for their favorite teams in the NCAA Tournament. This chaotic and thrilling event is known as March

Madness, a celebration of underdog stories, buzzer-beaters, and dreams coming true. While the tournament has had its share of unforgettable moments, one story stands out as the ultimate Cinderella tale: the 1983 NC State Wolfpack's miraculous run to the NCAA Championship. It's a story of hope, determination, and believing in the impossible.

The journey began in Raleigh, North Carolina, where the NC State Wolfpack basketball team entered the 1982–1983 season with high hopes. Led by head coach Jim Valvano, the team was talented but not considered among the nation's elite. They had a strong lineup that included Derrick Whittenburg, a sharpshooting guard; Sidney Lowe, their steady point guard; and Thurl Bailey, a towering forward with a knack for scoring. But the team faced stiff competition in the Atlantic Coast Conference (ACC), home to powerhouse programs like the University of North Carolina and the University of Virginia.

Early in the season, NC State showed flashes of brilliance, but their campaign was marred by injuries and inconsistency. Whittenburg, one of their star players, suffered a broken foot midway through the season, forcing him to miss several games. Without him, the team struggled, and their chances of making the NCAA Tournament began to fade. By the time the ACC Tournament rolled around, NC State needed a miracle just to qualify for the national tournament.

Jim Valvano, affectionately known as "Coach V," was an eternal optimist. He refused to let his players give up, even when the odds were against them. Valvano was as much a motivator as he was a coach, known for his infectious energy and ability to inspire belief. "Survive and advance," he told his players. That became their mantra—a reminder that all they needed to do was win the next game, no matter how daunting the challenge.

In the ACC Tournament, NC State's journey seemed destined to end quickly. They faced Wake Forest in the opening round, a team they had struggled against earlier in the season. But with Whittenburg back in the lineup, the Wolfpack found their rhythm. They defeated Wake Forest in a hard-fought game, then upset North Carolina in the semifinals, setting up a showdown with Virginia, led by the dominant 7'4" center Ralph Sampson, in the championship game. Against all odds, NC State pulled off another upset, securing the ACC Tournament title and earning an automatic bid to the NCAA Tournament.

Even with their ACC triumph, few believed NC State could make a deep run in the NCAA Tournament. They were seeded sixth in their region and faced a grueling path to the Final Four. But Coach Valvano's message remained the same: "Survive and advance."

In their opening game, the Wolfpack faced Pepperdine, and it quickly became clear that their tournament journey would be anything but easy.

The game went into double overtime, with NC State trailing late in the second extra period. But in the final seconds, the Wolfpack forced a turnover, and Thurl Bailey hit a clutch shot to give them the win. It was a narrow escape, but it kept their dream alive.

Next came a matchup against UNLV, one of the top teams in the country. UNLV's high-powered offense had dismantled opponents all season, and most expected them to overwhelm NC State. But the Wolfpack played with relentless energy, slowing the pace of the game and frustrating their opponents. Whittenburg and Bailey led the way, and NC State pulled off another stunning upset.

The victories kept coming, each one more improbable than the last. In the Sweet 16, they defeated Utah, and in the Elite Eight, they faced Virginia once again. Ralph Sampson loomed large, but NC State found a way to neutralize him, using a combination of tough defense and clutch shooting. With another upset victory, the Wolfpack punched their ticket to the Final Four.

By this point, the nation had taken notice. NC State's improbable run captured the hearts of fans everywhere, who began to believe in the magic of March Madness. The Wolfpack were no longer just a scrappy underdog; they were a symbol of hope, proving that anything was possible in the world of sports.

In the Final Four, NC State faced Georgia, a team that had also defied expectations to reach the national semifinals. The game was another nail-biter, with both teams trading baskets down the stretch. Once again, the Wolfpack found a way to win, advancing to the championship game to face the top-ranked Houston Cougars.

The Houston Cougars were a juggernaut. Nicknamed "Phi Slama Jama" for their high-flying dunks and athleticism, they were led by future NBA stars Hakeem Olajuwon and Clyde Drexler. Houston had steamrolled through the tournament, and most experts predicted they would dominate NC State in the championship game. But the Wolfpack weren't intimidated. They had come too far to back down now.

On April 4, 1983, the championship game tipped off in Albuquerque, New Mexico. From the start, it was clear that NC State's strategy was to slow the game down and keep Houston from running away with it. The Wolfpack played deliberate, patient basketball, forcing the Cougars into a half-court game. Their defense was relentless, and their offense, though not flashy, was efficient.

The game remained close throughout, with neither team able to pull away. In the final minutes, the tension was almost unbearable. With less than a minute remaining, the score was tied at 52-52. Houston had the ball, but NC State's defense forced a turnover, giving the Wolfpack a chance to win. Valvano called a timeout to set up the final play.

As the clock ticked down, Whittenburg launched a desperation shot from well beyond the three-point line. The ball arced high into the air, and for a moment, it seemed like it would miss. But then, out of nowhere, Lorenzo Charles leapt up, caught the ball, and slammed it through the hoop as time expired. The crowd erupted in disbelief and joy. NC State had done it—they were national champions.

Coach Valvano sprinted onto the court, searching for someone to hug, his arms raised in triumph. The players celebrated, tears streaming down their faces as they embraced one another. It was a moment of pure joy and unbridled emotion, the culmination of an incredible journey.

NC State's miracle run remains one of the greatest stories in sports history. It wasn't just about basketball; it was about believing in yourself, overcoming adversity, and refusing to give up. The 1983 Wolfpack taught the world that dreams can come true, no matter how impossible they seem.

"Don't give up. Don't ever give up."

— **Jim Valvano**

LeBron James: The Kid from Akron

How Hard Work, Talent, and Dedication Turned a Boy from Ohio into a Basketball Legend

LeBron James is one of the most famous athletes in the world. Known as "The King," he has dominated basketball for decades, inspiring millions with his extraordinary talent, incredible work ethic, and dedication both on and off the court. But before the championship rings, MVP trophies, and global fame, LeBron was just a kid from Akron, Ohio, facing obstacles that could have stopped him from ever reaching his potential. This is the story of how a boy from humble beginnings rose to become one of the greatest basketball players of all time.

LeBron Raymone James was born on December 30, 1984, in Akron, Ohio, a small city not far from Cleveland. His mother, Gloria James, was just 16 years old when she gave birth to him. Life wasn't easy for the young family. Gloria struggled to provide for LeBron as a single parent, working multiple jobs to keep food on the table. They moved from one apartment to another, often in neighborhoods plagued by poverty and violence. Despite the hardships, Gloria made sure LeBron always felt loved and supported.

LeBron's early life was marked by instability. By the time he was in elementary school, he had already moved more than a dozen times. The constant upheaval made it difficult for him to focus on school and make friends. But even as a young boy, LeBron found joy in sports. Whether it was football, basketball, or just playing outside with neighborhood kids, he loved to compete. His natural athleticism stood out immediately, and people began to notice his potential.

When LeBron was nine years old, his life took a pivotal turn. Gloria made the difficult decision to let him live with Frank Walker, a local football coach who saw something special in LeBron and wanted to help him.

Frank introduced LeBron to organized sports, including basketball. It didn't take long for everyone to realize that basketball wasn't just a hobby for LeBron—it was his passion and his calling.

LeBron began playing for local youth teams, where his talent became undeniable. He had a unique combination of size, speed, and skill, but what really set him apart was his understanding of the game. Even as a child, LeBron had an almost magical ability to see plays develop before they happened. Coaches marveled at his basketball IQ, his unselfishness, and his ability to make everyone around him better.

As LeBron entered middle school, his star continued to rise. He joined a local travel basketball team called the Shooting Stars, where he played alongside his childhood friends Dru Joyce, Sian Cotton, and Willie McGee. The group became known as the "Fab Four," and together, they dominated youth basketball tournaments across the country. By the time LeBron reached high school, he was already being compared to some of the greatest players in the history of the game.

LeBron attended St. Vincent-St. Mary High School, a small Catholic school in Akron. As a freshman, he made the varsity basketball team, something almost unheard of for a 14-year-old. In his very first season, LeBron led the Fighting Irish to a state championship, averaging 18 points and 6 rebounds per game. His performances were electrifying, and it didn't take long for word to spread. Scouts, journalists, and even NBA players began showing up to watch this high school phenom.

Over the next three years, LeBron's legend grew. He led St. Vincent-St. Mary to three state championships in four years, dazzling fans with his athleticism, court vision, and ability to perform under pressure. By his junior year, he was being called "The Chosen One," a nickname that reflected the belief that he was destined to be one of the greatest players of all time. Sports Illustrated featured him on its cover, an almost unheard-of honor for a high school athlete.

But LeBron's journey wasn't without challenges. As his fame grew, so did the pressure. He was scrutinized in a way no teenager should have to endure, with reporters following his every move and critics questioning whether he could live up to the hype. LeBron handled the attention with remarkable maturity, focusing on his game and leaning on his close-knit group of friends for support. He always credited his mother, Gloria, for keeping him grounded and teaching him the importance of hard work and humility.

By the time LeBron graduated in 2003, he was a household name. The Cleveland Cavaliers selected him as the first overall pick in the NBA Draft, bringing him back to his home state of Ohio. At just 18 years old, LeBron was stepping onto the biggest stage in basketball, with the hopes of an entire city resting on his shoulders.

LeBron's impact was immediate. In his rookie season, he averaged 20.9 points, 5.5 rebounds, and 5.9 assists per game, earning the NBA Rookie of the Year award. Fans marveled at his ability to dominate games despite his youth and inexperience. Over the next few years, he continued to improve, leading the Cavaliers to the playoffs and earning his first MVP award in 2009. But as great as he was, there was one thing missing: a championship.

LeBron's decision to leave Cleveland in 2010 and join the Miami Heat sparked controversy and criticism. Many fans felt betrayed, but LeBron knew he needed to surround himself with other great players to achieve his ultimate goal. In Miami, he teamed up with Dwyane Wade and Chris Bosh to form a "superteam," and the move paid off. LeBron led the Heat to back-to-back championships in 2012 and 2013, finally cementing his status as a winner.

But LeBron's story didn't end there. In 2014, he returned to Cleveland with one goal: to bring his hometown its first NBA championship. The journey wasn't easy, but in 2016, LeBron delivered on his promise. In a historic NBA Finals against the Golden State Warriors, LeBron led the Cavaliers to a dramatic come-from-behind victory, overcoming a 3-1 series deficit to win the championship. His block on Andre Iguodala in Game 7 became one of the most iconic moments in NBA history.

LeBron's legacy extends far beyond basketball. Off the court, he has used his platform to make a difference in the world. In 2018, he opened the I PROMISE School in Akron, a public school for at-risk children that provides free tuition, meals, and support for families. He has been a vocal advocate for social justice, using his voice to fight for equality and inspire change.

LeBron James's story is one of talent, perseverance, and purpose. From his humble beginnings in Akron to the global stage of the NBA, he has shown that greatness isn't just about what you achieve—it's about how you inspire others along the way.

"Nothing is given. Everything is earned. You work for what you have."

— LeBron James

The Ice Bowl: Packers vs. Cowboys

How the Coldest Game in NFL History Became a Battle for the Ages

On December 31, 1967, the Green Bay Packers and Dallas Cowboys faced off in one of the most legendary games in NFL history. Known as "The Ice Bowl," this NFL Championship game was played in sub-zero temperatures at Lambeau Field in Green Bay, Wisconsin. It wasn't just a test of skill; it was a test of willpower, endurance, and determination. What unfolded that day became a symbol of grit and resilience, a game that would forever be etched into the annals of football history.

The Packers, coached by the legendary Vince Lombardi, had already established themselves as a dynasty. They had won three of the past five NFL Championships, and their disciplined, hard-nosed style of play made them one of the most respected teams in the league. Led by quarterback Bart Starr, the Packers were known for their precision offense and ferocious defense. Lombardi demanded excellence from his players, and they delivered time and again.

The Dallas Cowboys, coached by Tom Landry, were a rising power in the NFL. Known for their innovative strategies and athletic talent, the Cowboys were eager to dethrone the Packers and establish themselves as the new kings of football. Their quarterback, Don Meredith, led a dynamic offense, while their defense, nicknamed the "Doomsday Defense," was one of the toughest in the league. The stage was set for an epic showdown.

As game day approached, weather forecasts predicted bitterly cold conditions, but no one could have anticipated just how brutal it would be. On the morning of December 31, temperatures in Green Bay plummeted to -15°F (-26°C), with a wind chill that made it feel like -48°F (-44°C). It was so cold that referees couldn't use their whistles because they would freeze to their lips. Instead, they resorted to shouting and hand signals to officiate the game. Players' breath turned to ice, their cleats struggled to grip the frozen turf, and the leather football became hard as a rock.

Despite the extreme conditions, more than 50,000 fans packed into Lambeau Field, bundled in heavy coats, scarves, and blankets. Many had traveled long distances to witness the game, braving the frigid temperatures to cheer on their teams. The Ice Bowl wasn't just a football game—it was a test of human endurance, both for the players and the fans.

The game began with the Packers taking an early lead. On their first drive, Bart Starr connected with wide receiver Boyd Dowler for an eight-yard touchdown pass. The Packers' offense looked sharp despite the icy conditions, and the home crowd roared with excitement. But the Cowboys quickly responded, tying the game with a touchdown run by Dan Reeves. It was clear from the start that this would be a hard-fought battle.

As the first half progressed, the bitter cold took its toll. Players struggled to keep their hands warm enough to grip the ball, and linemen's helmets frosted over from their breath. The field, frozen solid, felt like concrete, making every tackle more punishing than usual. Yet both teams fought valiantly, trading blows in a game that was as much about mental toughness as it was about physical skill.

By halftime, the Packers led 14-10, but the Cowboys came out strong in the second half. In the third quarter, Dallas capitalized on a Green Bay turnover, with running back Lance Rentzel scoring a touchdown to give the Cowboys a 17-14 lead. The momentum had shifted, and the Packers found themselves on their heels.

The fourth quarter was a battle of attrition. Both teams struggled to move the ball as the cold continued to sap their energy. The Packers' offense, which had been so effective earlier in the game, began to falter. Time was running out, and Green Bay's hopes of winning a third consecutive championship seemed to be slipping away.

With just over four minutes remaining, the Packers regained possession of the ball on their own 32-yard line. Trailing by three points, they needed a miracle drive to win the game. Bart Starr, known for his calm under pressure, gathered his teammates in the huddle. "We can do this," he told them. "Stay focused, and we'll get it done."

What followed was one of the most remarkable drives in NFL history. Starr methodically led the Packers down the field, completing crucial passes and relying on running back Donny Anderson to gain tough yards on the ground. The frozen field made every play a challenge, but the

Packers refused to give up. With less than a minute remaining, they reached the Cowboys' 1-yard line.

The Packers called their final timeout with 16 seconds left on the clock. It was third down, and the game—and their championship hopes—hung in the balance. Lombardi and Starr discussed the next play on the sidelines. The original plan was to hand the ball off to Anderson, but Starr had a different idea. He suggested a quarterback sneak, a risky move given the icy conditions and the Cowboys' stout defensive line. Lombardi's response was classic: "Run it, and let's get the hell out of here."

Starr returned to the huddle and relayed the play to his teammates. As the Packers lined up for what would be the final play of the game, the tension in the stadium was palpable. The ball was snapped, and Starr lunged forward behind the blocking of guard Jerry Kramer and center Ken Bowman. The line surged, and Starr slipped into the end zone for the game-winning touchdown.

The crowd erupted in celebration as Starr was mobbed by his teammates. The Packers had done it. They had overcome the freezing temperatures, a tenacious opponent, and seemingly impossible odds to win the NFL Championship. The final score: Green Bay 21, Dallas 17.

The Ice Bowl was more than just a football game—it was a testament to the human spirit. The players who took the field that day endured conditions few could imagine, and their performance was a display of courage, resilience, and determination. For Bart Starr and the Packers, it was a crowning achievement, a moment that solidified their place as one of the greatest teams in NFL history.

The legacy of the Ice Bowl endures to this day. It remains one of the most iconic games in football history, a reminder of what can be achieved when people refuse to give up, no matter how challenging the circumstances. For fans, it is a story of heroism and perseverance, a symbol of what makes football—and sports in general—so special.

"It's not whether you get knocked down, it's whether you get up."

— Vince Lombardi

Tom Brady: The Comeback King

How a Sixth-Round Draft Pick Became the Greatest Quarterback in NFL History

Tom Brady's journey to becoming one of the greatest quarterbacks of all time is a story of perseverance, hard work, and an unyielding belief in himself. From being an overlooked sixth-round draft pick to leading historic comebacks in the biggest games, Brady's career has been defined by his ability to rise above challenges. Among his many incredible feats, one stands out as the ultimate testament to his greatness: the New England Patriots' historic comeback against the Atlanta Falcons in Super Bowl LI.

Tom Brady was born on August 3, 1977, in San Mateo, California. Growing up in a sports-loving family, he idolized Joe Montana, the legendary quarterback for the San Francisco 49ers. Brady spent countless hours watching 49ers games, dreaming of one day playing in the NFL. However, Brady's road to the league was anything but smooth. Unlike many future NFL stars, Brady wasn't a standout athlete in high school. He wasn't the fastest runner, the strongest thrower, or the most highly recruited player.

Despite these challenges, Brady earned a scholarship to the University of Michigan, where he joined the Wolverines football team. Even in college, Brady wasn't handed opportunities. He spent his first two seasons on the bench, watching other quarterbacks take the field. Frustrated but determined, Brady worked tirelessly to improve his game. By his junior year, he earned the starting quarterback position and began to show glimpses of his potential. However, even after leading Michigan to a series of victories, he wasn't considered a top NFL prospect.

In the 2000 NFL Draft, Brady's name wasn't called until the 199th overall pick in the sixth round. The New England Patriots selected him, but he was far from a sure thing. At the time, Brady was the team's fourth-string quarterback, buried on the depth chart and considered a long shot to make the roster. But Brady didn't let the doubters define him. He approached every practice with intensity, studying the playbook and proving himself through sheer effort and determination.

Brady's big break came in 2001 when Patriots starting quarterback Drew Bledsoe suffered a serious injury early in the season. Brady stepped in as the starter and never looked back. He led the Patriots to an improbable Super Bowl victory that year, earning his first championship ring and beginning what would become one of the most dominant dynasties in NFL history.

Over the next decade and a half, Brady established himself as one of the league's elite quarterbacks. His leadership, precision passing, and ability to perform in clutch situations set him apart. By the time the Patriots reached Super Bowl LI in February 2017, Brady had already won four Super Bowl titles and three MVP awards. Yet, even with his remarkable track record, no one could have predicted what was about to happen.

Super Bowl LI was held in Houston, Texas, and pitted the New England Patriots against the Atlanta Falcons. The Falcons were led by quarterback Matt Ryan, who had just won the NFL MVP award for his spectacular play that season. Atlanta's offense was explosive, featuring dynamic players like Julio Jones and Devonta Freeman, and their defense was young and aggressive. Many believed the Falcons had the firepower to dethrone the Patriots.

The game began disastrously for Brady and the Patriots. Atlanta's defense dominated the first half, forcing turnovers and shutting down New England's usually potent offense. Meanwhile, the Falcons' offense carved through the Patriots' defense with ease. By halftime, the Falcons had built a commanding 21-3 lead, leaving the Patriots stunned and their fans demoralized.

In the third quarter, things went from bad to worse. Atlanta extended their lead to 28-3 after a touchdown pass from Matt Ryan. At that moment, the game seemed all but over. No team in Super Bowl history had ever come back from a deficit larger than 10 points. Fans began leaving the stadium, convinced they had seen enough.

But on the Patriots' sideline, Tom Brady remained calm. He didn't yell, panic, or show frustration. Instead, he gathered his teammates and delivered a simple message: "We're not out of this. Let's do our jobs, one play at a time." Brady's unwavering confidence began to rub off on his teammates, who rallied around their leader.

The comeback began with a field goal late in the third quarter, trimming the deficit to 28-9. While the score seemed insignificant, it gave the Patriots a glimmer of hope. Early in the fourth quarter, Brady led a long drive that ended with a touchdown pass to running back James White. The Patriots then executed a two-point conversion, cutting the Falcons' lead to 28-17.

Suddenly, the momentum began to shift. The Falcons' high-powered offense, which had been unstoppable in the first half, started to falter. The Patriots' defense tightened up, forcing key turnovers and giving Brady more opportunities to work his magic. With just under six minutes left in the game, Brady orchestrated another scoring drive, capped by a touchdown pass to Danny Amendola. Another successful two-point conversion brought the Patriots within three points, 28-25.

By now, the stadium was roaring with excitement. The once-insurmountable lead had all but evaporated, and the Falcons were reeling. On their next possession, Matt Ryan and the Falcons appeared to be in position to seal the game after a spectacular catch by Julio Jones put them in field goal range. But a critical sack and a holding penalty pushed them back, forcing a punt and giving the ball back to Brady with just over two minutes remaining.

With the game on the line, Brady delivered one of the greatest drives in NFL history. He methodically marched the Patriots down the field, completing pass after pass with pinpoint accuracy. The Falcons' defense, exhausted and overwhelmed, had no answer for Brady's brilliance. As time expired, the Patriots kicked a field goal to tie the game, sending the Super Bowl into overtime for the first time ever.

In overtime, the Patriots won the coin toss and elected to receive the ball. Brady, now fully in control, led the Patriots on a game-winning drive. Facing a defense that had been on the field for nearly the entire second half, Brady dissected the Falcons with surgical precision. The drive culminated in a two-yard touchdown run by James White, completing the greatest comeback in Super Bowl history. The final score: Patriots 34, Falcons 28.

Brady's performance in Super Bowl LI was nothing short of legendary. He set Super Bowl records for completions (43) and passing yards (466) while engineering the largest comeback in the game's history. It was a masterclass in leadership, resilience, and determination, further cementing Brady's status as the greatest quarterback of all time.

The victory was about more than just a championship. It was a testament to Brady's unshakable belief in himself and his teammates. Even when the odds were stacked against them, Brady refused to quit. His ability to inspire those around him and execute under pressure made the impossible possible.

Today, Tom Brady's career is a shining example of what can be achieved through hard work, preparation, and perseverance. From a sixth-round draft pick to a seven-time Super Bowl champion, Brady's journey is proof that greatness isn't given—it's earned.

"You have to believe in the process. You have to believe in what you're doing. You have to believe in the people around you."

— Tom Brady

Walter Payton's Heart of a Champion

How "Sweetness" Inspired the World with Talent, Dedication, and Compassion

Walter Payton wasn't just a football player; he was a symbol of perseverance, excellence, and heart. Known as "Sweetness" for his smooth playing style and kind demeanor, Payton is widely regarded as one of the greatest running backs in NFL history. But his legacy extends far beyond the football field. Through his relentless work ethic, his commitment to his team, and his dedication to making a difference off the field, Payton became a hero whose story continues to inspire.

Walter Jerry Payton was born on July 25, 1954, in Columbia, Mississippi. He grew up during a time of intense racial segregation, in a small town where opportunities for African Americans were limited. Despite the challenges, Payton had a joyful childhood, surrounded by his close-knit family. He was an active, playful boy who loved to sing in his church choir and play sports with his friends. His older brother Eddie was a talented athlete, and Walter often followed in his footsteps, determined to keep up.

Payton's introduction to organized football came later than most. He didn't join his high school team until his junior year, focusing instead on other sports like basketball and track. But once he stepped onto the football field, it was clear he had found his calling. Payton's natural athleticism, combined with his competitive spirit, made him a standout player. By his senior year, he was a star at Jefferson High School, known for his explosive speed, incredible balance, and ability to break tackles.

After high school, Payton attended Jackson State University, a historically Black college in Mississippi. There, he quickly established himself as one of the best players in college football. Over four seasons, he set numerous records, including 65 career touchdowns. Payton's dominance on the field earned him national attention, and in 1975, the Chicago Bears selected him with the fourth overall pick in the NFL Draft.

Payton's transition to the NFL wasn't easy. The Bears were struggling as a franchise, with losing seasons and a lack of talent on the roster. Payton knew he would face challenges, but he embraced them with his signature work ethic and positive attitude. From the beginning, he committed himself to being the best player he could be, both for his team and for himself.

Payton's training regimen was legendary. He pushed his body to its limits, running up steep hills, lifting weights, and practicing relentlessly. He was determined to outwork everyone, believing that effort and preparation were the keys to success. His hard work paid off. By his second season, Payton was one of the most dominant running backs in the league. He ran with a unique combination of power, speed, and agility, earning the respect of teammates and opponents alike.

In 1977, Payton had one of the greatest seasons in NFL history. He rushed for 1,852 yards, including a single-game record of 275 yards against the Minnesota Vikings—a record that stood for decades. Payton's performances earned him the NFL MVP award, and he became the face of the Chicago Bears. But despite his individual success, the Bears continued to struggle as a team, missing the playoffs year after year.

For Payton, football wasn't just about personal achievements; it was about winning as a team. He remained committed to the Bears, working tirelessly to improve and inspire his teammates. His leadership and unselfishness were evident both on and off the field. Payton was known for his sense of humor, his generosity, and his ability to lift the spirits of those around him. He treated every teammate, coach, and fan with kindness and respect, embodying the nickname "Sweetness."

In 1985, Payton's dedication was finally rewarded. The Bears assembled one of the greatest teams in NFL history, led by a dominant defense known as the "Monsters of the Midway." With Payton as their offensive anchor, the Bears stormed through the regular season with a 15-1 record. In the playoffs, they crushed their opponents, earning a spot in Super Bowl XX.

The Super Bowl was the culmination of Payton's career. Although he didn't have a standout game statistically—he was used primarily as a decoy to open up opportunities for other players—his contributions were vital to the team's success. The Bears defeated the New England Patriots 46-10, capturing their first Super Bowl title. Payton celebrated with his teammates, grateful for the opportunity to achieve his lifelong dream.

After 13 seasons in the NFL, Payton retired in 1987 as the league's all-time leading rusher, with 16,726 yards. His records, which included 110 rushing touchdowns and nine Pro Bowl selections, cemented his status as one of the greatest players in history. But Payton's legacy wasn't just about numbers. He was admired for his toughness, his humility, and his unwavering commitment to excellence.

Off the field, Payton dedicated himself to helping others. He was deeply involved in charity work, supporting causes like education, youth programs, and organ donation. He believed in using his platform to make a difference, and he inspired countless people with his generosity and compassion.

In 1999, Payton was diagnosed with a rare liver disease called primary sclerosing cholangitis. Despite his illness, he remained positive and determined, using his diagnosis to raise awareness about the importance of organ donation. Payton's bravery during his final months was a reflection of the character he displayed throughout his life.

Walter Payton passed away on November 1, 1999, at the age of 45. His death was a profound loss for the football world and for everyone who had been touched by his kindness and generosity. In honor of his legacy, the NFL established the Walter Payton Man of the Year Award, given annually to a player who demonstrates excellence on the field and in their community.

Walter Payton's story is one of perseverance, heart, and the belief that greatness comes not just from talent, but from how you use it to impact others. His example continues to inspire athletes, fans, and anyone striving to make a difference in the world.

"When you're good at something, you'll tell everyone. When you're great at something, they'll tell you."

— Walter Payton

The Hand of God and the Goal of the Century

How Diego Maradona Made History in the 1986 World Cup

Few moments in sports have captured the imagination of fans like Diego Maradona's performance in the quarterfinal match of the 1986 FIFA World Cup. Facing England in a game filled with political tension and

72

historic rivalry, Maradona delivered two of the most iconic goals in soccer history. One was shrouded in controversy, the other hailed as the greatest goal ever scored. Together, they became symbols of Maradona's genius and cemented his legacy as one of the greatest players the game has ever seen.

Diego Maradona was born on October 30, 1960, in Villa Fiorito, a shantytown on the outskirts of Buenos Aires, Argentina. Growing up in poverty, young Diego fell in love with soccer at an early age. From the moment he first kicked a ball, it was clear he had a rare gift. His quick feet, incredible balance, and unparalleled vision made him stand out, even among older kids. By the time he was ten years old, Maradona was a local sensation, dazzling crowds with his skills for a youth team called Los Cebollitas.

Maradona's talent took him far from Villa Fiorito. By the age of 16, he had made his debut for Argentinos Juniors, a top-flight club in Argentina. His performances were electrifying, and it wasn't long before he was called up to the national team. At just 17, he narrowly missed being selected for the 1978 World Cup squad, but his time would come. Four years later, Maradona played in the 1982 World Cup, showcasing flashes of brilliance but ultimately falling short of expectations. By 1986, he was determined to make his mark on the world's biggest stage.

The 1986 World Cup was held in Mexico, and Maradona entered the tournament as Argentina's captain and undisputed star. He was at the peak of his powers, a player capable of turning any game with a moment of magic. In the group stages, he demonstrated his dominance, leading Argentina to victories over South Korea and Bulgaria. His creativity, leadership, and relentless drive made him the focal point of the team. But it was in the quarterfinal against England where Maradona's legend would be born.

The match took place on June 22, 1986, at the Estadio Azteca in Mexico City. The stakes were enormous. Argentina and England had a storied rivalry, intensified by the Falklands War just four years earlier. For many Argentinians, this game was about more than soccer—it was a chance to reclaim pride on the world stage. The tension was palpable as the teams took the field, and the eyes of the world were on Maradona.

The first half was a hard-fought battle, with both teams creating chances but failing to score. The game was physical and intense, with every pass and tackle carrying the weight of the nations' histories. Then, six minutes into the second half, the moment came that would define the match—and Maradona's career.

Maradona received the ball just outside the penalty box and attempted a pass to a teammate. The ball deflected off an English defender and looped into the air. Maradona, standing near England's goalkeeper, Peter

Shilton, leaped to meet the ball. At just 5'5", Maradona was no match for the 6'1" Shilton in an aerial duel. But as the ball descended, Maradona extended his left hand and punched it into the net. The English players immediately protested, but the referee, unable to see the infraction clearly, allowed the goal to stand.

After the game, Maradona would famously describe the play as "a little with the head of Maradona and a little with the hand of God." The "Hand of God" goal became one of the most controversial moments in sports history, dividing fans and sparking debates that continue to this day. For Argentinians, it was a moment of cleverness and cunning, a triumph of the underdog. For the English, it was an unforgivable act of dishonesty. But for Maradona, it was just the beginning.

Just four minutes later, Maradona delivered what many consider the greatest goal in soccer history. Receiving the ball in his own half, he embarked on a breathtaking solo run. Maradona weaved through the English defense, evading tackle after tackle with astonishing speed and skill. He danced past five defenders, leaving them helpless in his wake, before rounding Shilton and calmly slotting the ball into the net. The goal was a masterpiece, a perfect blend of athleticism, creativity, and composure. Even the English fans couldn't help but admire its brilliance.

The contrast between the two goals—one controversial, the other sublime—captured the essence of Maradona. He was a player who could break the rules and then rewrite them, a genius whose flaws only added to his mystique. The rest of the match was a formality. England managed to score a late goal, but Argentina held on for a 2-1 victory, advancing to the semifinals. Maradona was carried off the field by his teammates, celebrated as a hero.

Argentina went on to win the World Cup, defeating Belgium in the semifinals and West Germany in the final. Maradona was the tournament's undisputed star, scoring five goals and assisting on five others. His performance in 1986 is widely regarded as one of the greatest in World Cup history, and his contributions to Argentina's victory made him a national icon.

But Maradona's story didn't end with the World Cup. He continued to play at the highest level, dazzling fans with his skills and passion. Yet his career was also marked by struggles, including battles with addiction and controversies both on and off the field. Despite these challenges, Maradona's impact on the game remains unparalleled.

Diego Maradona passed away on November 25, 2020, at the age of 60, but his legacy endures. The "Hand of God" and the "Goal of the Century" are immortalized in the memories of soccer fans, symbols of a player who could create magic on the field and inspire millions around the world.

"To see the ball, to run after it, makes me the happiest man in the world."

— Diego Maradona

The U.S. Women's National Team Wins the 1999 World Cup

How a Team of Trailblazers Inspired a Nation

On a hot summer day in July 1999, over 90,000 fans packed the Rose Bowl in Pasadena, California, to witness a moment that would change the landscape of women's sports forever. The U.S. Women's National Soccer Team (USWNT) was competing in the final of the FIFA Women's World Cup against China in what would become one of the most iconic moments in sports history. The journey to that day, however, was filled with hard work, sacrifice, and a determination to prove that women's soccer could captivate the world.

The story begins years earlier, when women's soccer was still fighting for recognition. The U.S. women's program was officially established in the mid-1980s, but it lacked the resources and support enjoyed by the men's team. Despite the challenges, the early players were passionate about the game and determined to succeed. They played not for fame or fortune, but for the love of soccer and the hope of inspiring future generations.

In 1991, the USWNT won the inaugural Women's World Cup, held in China. Despite their triumph, the victory received little media attention back home. Women's soccer was still seen as a niche sport, and the players often had to hold second jobs to make ends meet. But the 1991 win was a spark, and over the next eight years, the team worked tirelessly to grow the sport and prepare for the next opportunity to shine on the world stage.

By 1999, the U.S. team was a powerhouse. Led by head coach Tony DiCicco, the roster featured a mix of veteran stars and rising talents.

Players like Mia Hamm, Michelle Akers, Brandi Chastain, Kristine Lilly, and goalkeeper Briana Scurry were household names among soccer fans, known for their skill, leadership, and unrelenting drive. As the host nation for the 1999 World Cup, the team felt an enormous responsibility to represent their country and elevate women's sports.

The tournament began with high expectations and growing excitement. The U.S. team opened with a dominant 3-0 victory over Denmark, followed by wins against Nigeria and North Korea to top their group. Their style of play was electrifying—fast, creative, and full of heart. Fans quickly took notice, and stadiums filled with cheering crowds, many of them young girls inspired by the players' talent and determination.

In the quarterfinals, the U.S. faced Germany, one of the tournament favorites. It was a hard-fought match, with both teams displaying incredible skill and resilience. The U.S. overcame an early own goal to win 3-2, with goals from Tiffeny Milbrett and Kristine Lilly and an inspiring team effort that showcased their ability to rise under pressure.

The semifinals brought a showdown with Brazil, another soccer powerhouse. The match was physical and intense, but the U.S. prevailed 2-0, thanks to goals from Cindy Parlow and Mia Hamm. The victory secured their place in the final and set the stage for an unforgettable clash with China.

The final, held on July 10, 1999, was more than just a soccer game—it was a cultural moment. Over 90,000 fans packed the Rose Bowl, making it the largest crowd ever to attend a women's sporting event. Millions more tuned in from around the world, captivated by the energy and significance of the occasion. For the players, it was an opportunity to prove that women's sports could command the same level of attention and respect as men's.

China was a formidable opponent. Their team was disciplined, technically skilled, and physically strong, led by standout players like Sun Wen, who was later named FIFA Player of the Century. The U.S. knew they were in for a battle, and the game lived up to the hype. For 90 minutes of regulation time and 30 minutes of extra time, the two teams fought fiercely, neither able to break the 0-0 deadlock. Both defenses were rock-solid, and every shot, pass, and save carried enormous weight.

One of the defining moments of the match came in extra time, when Kristine Lilly made a crucial defensive play. China earned a corner kick, and their header seemed destined for the back of the net. But Lilly, stationed on the goal line, leapt up and cleared the ball with her head, saving the U.S. from conceding a late goal. It was a testament to the team's grit and determination to fight for every inch.

With the score still tied after 120 minutes, the championship would be decided by a penalty shootout—a nerve-wracking scenario where every kick could mean glory or heartbreak. The U.S. players lined up, their faces a mix of focus and determination. Briana Scurry, the team's goalkeeper, prepared herself for the biggest moments of her career.

China went first, and Sun Wen converted her penalty with ease. Carla Overbeck, the U.S. captain, stepped up next and calmly scored to level the shootout. The pressure continued to mount as both teams traded successful penalties. Then came the turning point. With the score tied at 2-2, Scurry made a diving save on China's third penalty, giving the U.S. an edge. It was a moment of brilliance that sent the crowd into a frenzy.

The shootout continued, with both teams converting their next penalties. Finally, it was Brandi Chastain's turn. The score was 4-4, and if she scored, the U.S. would win the World Cup. Chastain walked to the penalty spot, her heart pounding but her mind focused. She placed the ball, took a deep breath, and struck it with her left foot. The ball sailed into the top corner of the net, past the outstretched arms of the Chinese goalkeeper.

The stadium erupted in celebration as Chastain ripped off her jersey and dropped to her knees, fists clenched in triumph. The image of her ecstatic celebration became one of the most iconic photographs in sports history, symbolizing not just the victory, but the empowerment of women in sports.

The U.S. Women's National Team had done more than win a World Cup—they had inspired a nation. Their triumph resonated far beyond the soccer field, sparking a surge in interest in women's sports and empowering girls around the world to dream big. The players became role models, ambassadors, and pioneers, using their platform to advocate for equality and opportunity.

Today, the 1999 World Cup remains a landmark moment in sports history. It showcased the beauty of the game, the strength of teamwork, and the power of believing in something bigger than yourself. For the players, it was a culmination of years of hard work and sacrifice. For the fans, it was a celebration of what's possible when determination meets opportunity.

"Success isn't about the final result—it's about the journey and the belief that you can achieve greatness together."

— Brandi Chastain

Lionel Messi's First World Cup Win

How a Legendary Career Reached Its Pinnacle in Qatar 2022

For nearly two decades, Lionel Messi has been one of the most iconic and talented players in the history of soccer. From his dazzling dribbles to his unmatched playmaking, Messi has brought joy to millions of fans around the world. Yet, for much of his career, there was one glaring absence on his résumé: a FIFA World Cup trophy. In 2022, that changed forever. Messi's journey to his first World Cup victory wasn't just about lifting a trophy—it was a testament to perseverance, leadership, and the power of dreams.

Lionel Andrés Messi was born on June 24, 1987, in Rosario, Argentina. From a young age, it was clear he was destined for greatness. He grew up playing soccer in his neighborhood, often dribbling circles around kids much older than him. His talent was unmistakable, and at just six years old, he joined the youth academy of his local club, Newell's Old Boys. By the time he was eight, Messi was already a sensation, scoring goals at will and mesmerizing crowds with his skills.

But Messi's journey was far from smooth. At age 10, he was diagnosed with a growth hormone deficiency that threatened to derail his career. His family struggled to afford the treatment, and his future in soccer looked uncertain. Then came a lifeline: FC Barcelona, one of Europe's biggest clubs, offered to pay for Messi's medical expenses if he joined their youth academy. In 2000, Messi and his family moved to Spain, where he began training at La Masia, Barcelona's renowned academy.

Messi's rise through the ranks was meteoric. By the time he was 17, he had made his first-team debut for Barcelona, and it wasn't long before he became the centerpiece of the team. Over the next decade, Messi led Barcelona to unprecedented success, winning multiple league titles and

Champions League trophies. His individual accolades piled up as well, including a record number of Ballon d'Or awards, given annually to the world's best player.

While Messi's club career was unmatched, his time with the Argentine national team was more complicated. Argentina, a country with a rich soccer history, had not won a World Cup since 1986, when Diego Maradona led them to glory. Messi was often compared to Maradona, and fans dreamed of him bringing home another title. Yet, despite his brilliance, Messi and Argentina suffered repeated heartbreaks. They lost in the finals of the 2014 World Cup and two consecutive Copa América finals in 2015 and 2016. The losses weighed heavily on Messi, and in 2016, he briefly announced his retirement from international soccer, only to return months later.

The road to the 2022 World Cup in Qatar was filled with hope and determination. Messi, now 35, was nearing the end of his career, and many believed this would be his last chance to win the sport's ultimate prize. The Argentine team had grown stronger under coach Lionel Scaloni, with a mix of experienced veterans and rising stars like Julián Álvarez and Enzo Fernández. They entered the tournament as one of the favorites, bolstered by their victory in the 2021 Copa América, where Messi had finally won his first major international trophy.

The tournament began with a shocking setback. In their opening match, Argentina lost 2-1 to Saudi Arabia, despite Messi scoring an early penalty. The defeat sent shockwaves through the soccer world and put Argentina's World Cup hopes in jeopardy. But Messi and his teammates didn't panic. They regrouped, determined to show their true potential.

In their next match, Argentina faced Mexico in a must-win game. For much of the match, the Mexican defense held strong, but in the 64th minute, Messi broke through. From outside the penalty box, he unleashed a low, powerful shot that found the bottom corner of the net. The goal sparked Argentina to a 2-0 victory, reigniting their World Cup campaign. They followed it up with another 2-0 win over Poland, securing their place in the knockout rounds.

In the Round of 16, Argentina faced Australia. Messi was at his brilliant best, scoring the opening goal with a deft touch and mesmerizing the Australian defense throughout the match. Argentina won 2-1, advancing to the quarterfinals, where they faced the Netherlands in one of the tournament's most dramatic games.

The quarterfinal was a rollercoaster of emotions. Argentina took a 2-0 lead, with Messi providing a stunning assist for the first goal and scoring a penalty for the second. But the Netherlands mounted a late comeback, equalizing in the final minutes of regular time. The match went to a penalty shootout, and once again, Messi's leadership shone through. He converted his penalty, and goalkeeper Emiliano Martínez made crucial saves to secure Argentina's victory.

In the semifinals, Argentina faced Croatia, a team known for their resilience and discipline. Messi delivered another masterclass, scoring a penalty and providing a jaw-dropping assist for Julián Álvarez's goal. Argentina won 3-0, booking their place in the final against defending champions France.

The final, played on December 18, 2022, was a spectacle for the ages. The match pitted Messi against Kylian Mbappé, France's young superstar and Messi's teammate at Paris Saint-Germain. Argentina dominated the first half, taking a 2-0 lead with goals from Messi and Ángel Di María. But France roared back in the second half, with Mbappé scoring twice in quick succession to level the game at 2-2.

In extra time, Messi scored again, putting Argentina ahead 3-2. But the drama wasn't over. Mbappé completed his hat-trick with a penalty, sending the game to a nerve-wracking shootout. As the world watched with bated breath, Messi stepped up and coolly converted his penalty. Martínez made crucial saves, and Gonzalo Montiel scored the winning penalty, giving Argentina a 4-2 shootout victory.

The final whistle unleashed a wave of emotion. Messi fell to his knees, tears streaming down his face as his teammates rushed to embrace him.

The crowd erupted in celebration, chanting his name. After years of heartbreak and near misses, Messi had finally achieved his dream. He lifted the World Cup trophy high above his head, surrounded by his teammates, as fireworks lit up the Qatari sky.

For Argentina, the victory was a unifying moment, a celebration of their soccer heritage and the player who had brought them so much joy. For Messi, it was the crowning achievement of an extraordinary career, a testament to his perseverance and greatness.

Lionel Messi's first World Cup win is more than just a sports story—it's a tale of resilience, leadership, and the power of dreams. It reminds us that even the greatest face challenges, and that true greatness lies in the ability to rise above them.

"You have to fight to reach your dream. You have to sacrifice and work hard for it."

— **Lionel Messi**

Bo Jackson: The Greatest Two-Sport Athlete

How an Unstoppable Force Dominated Both Baseball and Football

When people hear the name Bo Jackson, they think of unparalleled athleticism, raw power, and jaw-dropping feats of strength and speed. He wasn't just a star in one sport—he was a legend in two. From hitting towering home runs on the baseball diamond to breaking tackles and outrunning defenders on the football field, Bo Jackson redefined what it meant to be an athlete. His story is one of natural talent, relentless drive, and a lasting impact on sports culture.

Vincent Edward "Bo" Jackson was born on November 30, 1962, in Bessemer, Alabama, the eighth of ten children in a working-class family. Life in Bessemer wasn't easy, but Bo's athletic ability was apparent from a young age. As a child, he seemed to have boundless energy and strength, earning the nickname "Bo" after a character in his favorite childhood stories who was always up to something mischievous.

Growing up, Bo excelled in every sport he tried. By the time he reached McAdory High School, he was a standout in football, baseball, and track. On the football field, Bo was unstoppable, scoring touchdowns with a mix of brute force and blistering speed. In baseball, his powerful swing and cannon of an arm made him a force to be reckoned with. And on the track, he set state records in the decathlon and 100-meter dash. It was clear that Bo Jackson wasn't just another athlete—he was something special.

After graduating high school, Bo accepted a scholarship to Auburn University, where he became one of the most dominant athletes in college sports history. In football, he was a game-changer. Bo's speed—clocked at an incredible 4.12 seconds in the 40-yard dash—was almost unfair for a running back his size. He could plow through defenders with his strength or simply outrun them with his speed. During his time at Auburn, Bo amassed more than 4,300 rushing yards, won the prestigious Heisman Trophy in 1985, and left a trail of highlight-reel plays that cemented his place as one of the greatest college football players of all time.

But football wasn't the only sport where Bo shined. He also played baseball for Auburn and quickly established himself as one of the top prospects in the nation. Scouts marveled at his ability to hit home runs with ease and cover ground in the outfield like a seasoned professional. Bo's performances on the diamond showed he wasn't just a football player dabbling in baseball—he was a legitimate two-sport star.

In 1986, Bo Jackson's future took an unexpected turn. The Tampa Bay Buccaneers selected him as the first overall pick in the NFL Draft, but a misunderstanding during the pre-draft process led to Bo feeling disrespected by the team. Instead of signing with Tampa Bay, Bo decided to pursue a career in Major League Baseball, signing with the Kansas City Royals.

Bo quickly made an impact in baseball. In 1987, during his first full season with the Royals, he hit 22 home runs and stole 10 bases. But Bo wasn't content with dominating just one sport. In 1987, the Los Angeles Raiders of the NFL came calling, and Bo agreed to join the team under one condition: he would play football only after the baseball season ended.

Balancing two professional sports was unprecedented, but Bo Jackson made it look effortless. In the fall, he suited up for the Raiders, where his combination of speed, power, and agility made him one of the most dangerous players in the NFL. In the spring and summer, he returned to the Royals, continuing to crush baseballs and make jaw-dropping plays in the outfield.

One of Bo's most iconic moments came in 1989, during the MLB All-Star Game. Facing one of baseball's top pitchers, Rick Reuschel, Bo led off the game with a mammoth home run to center field. The shot left fans and players in awe and earned him the All-Star Game MVP award. That same year, Bo hit 32 home runs and drove in 105 RBIs, solidifying his place as one of baseball's elite players.

Later that year, Bo had another unforgettable moment on the football field. In a Monday Night Football game against the Seattle Seahawks, Bo took a handoff and sprinted 91 yards for a touchdown, leaving defenders in the dust. The play was a perfect showcase of his blazing speed and raw power, and it remains one of the most replayed highlights in NFL history.

By the late 1980s, Bo Jackson wasn't just an athlete—he was a cultural phenomenon. In 1989, Nike launched the now-famous "Bo Knows" advertising campaign, which featured Bo excelling in a variety of sports, from basketball to hockey to tennis. The commercials captured Bo's larger-than-life persona and introduced him to a global audience. He became one of the most marketable athletes in the world, with his face plastered on magazine covers, posters, and TV screens.

For all his success, Bo Jackson's career was tragically cut short. In January 1991, during a playoff game against the Cincinnati Bengals, Bo suffered a devastating hip injury while being tackled. The injury was so severe that it ended his football career and threatened his ability to walk, let alone play professional sports. Doctors diagnosed him with a condition called avascular necrosis, which caused the bone tissue in his hip to die due to lack of blood flow.

Many believed Bo's athletic career was over. But true to his character, Bo refused to give up. After extensive rehabilitation and surgery, he made an improbable comeback to baseball in 1993, signing with the Chicago White Sox. Although he was no longer the same player physically, Bo continued to inspire fans with his determination and resilience. In his first at-bat back, he hit a home run, proving that his spirit was unbreakable.

Bo Jackson retired from professional sports in 1994, but his legacy remains unmatched. He is the only athlete in history to be named an All-Star in both Major League Baseball and the NFL. His ability to dominate two sports at the highest level is a feat that has never been replicated and likely never will be.

Beyond his athletic achievements, Bo is remembered for his humility and generosity. Despite his fame, he remained grounded, often giving back to his community and mentoring young athletes. Today, he is involved in various charitable endeavors and continues to inspire new generations with his story.

Bo Jackson's career was a reminder of the extraordinary potential of human athleticism. He showed the world that limits are meant to be shattered and that greatness comes not just from talent, but from a relentless drive to excel.

"Set your goals high, and don't stop till you get there."

— Bo Jackson

Simone Biles: The Queen of Gymnastics

Overcoming Adversity to Redefine Greatness

Simone Biles is more than a gymnast; she is a global icon of resilience, excellence, and the pursuit of greatness. Widely regarded as the greatest gymnast of all time, Biles has revolutionized her sport with her unparalleled skill, strength, and artistry. But her journey to the top wasn't just about medals and records. It was a story of overcoming adversity, confronting personal struggles, and redefining what it means to be a champion.

Simone Biles was born on March 14, 1997, in Columbus, Ohio. Her childhood was marked by challenges. Her mother, who struggled with substance abuse, was unable to care for Simone and her three siblings. By the time Simone was three, she and her younger sister, Adria, were placed in foster care. Despite the uncertainty and instability of her early years, Simone's natural energy and curiosity shone through.

In 2003, Simone's grandparents, Ron and Nellie Biles, stepped in to adopt her and Adria, providing them with the stability and love they needed to thrive. The family moved to Spring, Texas, where Simone's new life began to take shape. Ron and Nellie became Simone's biggest supporters, encouraging her to dream big and work hard.

Simone's introduction to gymnastics came during a daycare field trip when she was six years old. While other children played and ran around, Simone found herself mesmerized by the gymnasts practicing on beams and vaults. A coach noticed her natural strength and flexibility and suggested she join a gymnastics class. From that moment, Simone's passion for the sport took root.

By age eight, Simone was training with Aimee Boorman, the coach who would guide her through much of her career. Her talent was undeniable, and she quickly rose through the ranks of junior gymnastics. What set Simone apart wasn't just her incredible athleticism but her ability to perform skills that few others dared to try. She had a unique combination of power and grace, coupled with a work ethic that left her coaches in awe.

Simone's breakthrough came in 2013 when she won her first U.S. National Championship as a senior gymnast. At just 16 years old, she outperformed seasoned competitors, showing the world she was a force to be reckoned with. Later that year, she won her first World Championship, becoming the first African American woman to claim the all-around title. It was the beginning of a dominance that would redefine the sport.

Between 2013 and 2016, Simone became nearly unbeatable. She won three consecutive World Championship all-around titles, earning a reputation as the best gymnast on the planet. Her routines featured skills so difficult that they were often named after her, including the now-famous "Biles," a double layout with a half twist. No one else could match her combination of difficulty and execution.

The 2016 Olympics in Rio de Janeiro cemented Simone's status as a global superstar. She entered the Games as the heavy favorite and delivered one of the most dominant performances in Olympic history. Simone won four gold medals—in the all-around, team, vault, and floor exercise—and a bronze on the balance beam. Her all-around victory was particularly stunning, as she outscored the silver medalist by a margin rarely seen in such a competitive field.

But Simone's success wasn't just about winning. She inspired millions with her joy, humility, and infectious personality. Fans around the world were drawn to her story of perseverance and the way she carried herself with grace, even under immense pressure. For young girls, especially those of color, Simone became a role model and proof that they could achieve greatness in any arena.

After Rio, Simone took a year off from gymnastics, but her return in 2018 proved she hadn't missed a beat. She won another World Championship all-around title, bringing her total to four, and continued to push the boundaries of what was possible in gymnastics. Her routines grew even more difficult, and she consistently performed skills that other gymnasts wouldn't attempt.

While Simone's dominance on the mat was unmatched, her life off the mat presented its own challenges. In 2018, she came forward as one of the hundreds of athletes who had been abused by former USA Gymnastics doctor Larry Nassar. Speaking out took tremendous courage, and Simone became a powerful advocate for change within the sport.

She demanded accountability from USA Gymnastics and worked to ensure that future generations of athletes would be better protected.

By 2021, Simone was preparing for the Tokyo Olympics, where she was expected to continue her reign as the best gymnast in the world. But when the Games arrived, Simone faced an unexpected challenge: her mental health. During the team competition, she struggled to find her focus and experienced a phenomenon known as the "twisties," a mental block that makes it difficult for gymnasts to orient themselves in the air. It was a dangerous condition that could lead to serious injury.

Rather than push through and risk her safety, Simone made the difficult decision to withdraw from several events. Her choice sparked a global conversation about mental health in sports and the pressure faced by elite athletes. Some criticized her for stepping back, but many more praised her bravery in prioritizing her well-being over competition.

Despite the setbacks, Simone returned to compete in the balance beam final, where she earned a bronze medal. Her performance was a reminder of her resilience and her ability to rise above challenges. While the Tokyo Games didn't go as planned, they became a defining moment in Simone's career—proof that being a champion isn't just about winning but about staying true to yourself.

Simone's legacy extends far beyond her record-breaking achievements. She has inspired a generation of athletes to dream big and speak out for what they believe in. Her advocacy for mental health, combined with her unparalleled skill and grace, has made her a trailblazer in every sense of the word.

Today, Simone Biles is more than the greatest gymnast of all time. She is a symbol of courage, perseverance, and the power of believing in yourself. Her story continues to inspire, showing the world that true greatness comes from overcoming adversity and using your platform to make a difference.

"I'm not the next Usain Bolt or Michael Phelps. I'm the first Simone Biles."

— **Simone Biles**

Usain Bolt: The Lightning Bolt's Record-Breaking Speed

The Rise of the Fastest Man Alive

In the world of track and field, no name resonates like Usain Bolt. The Jamaican sprinter captivated the world with his record-breaking speed, electrifying charisma, and larger-than-life personality. Dubbed "The Lightning Bolt," Bolt didn't just dominate his sport—he redefined it, becoming the standard by which all sprinters are now measured. His journey to becoming the fastest man alive is a tale of extraordinary talent, relentless determination, and an infectious love for competition.

Usain St. Leo Bolt was born on August 21, 1986, in Sherwood Content, a small village in Trelawny, Jamaica. Growing up, Bolt was like many other Jamaican children—energetic, mischievous, and obsessed with sports. He spent hours playing cricket and soccer with his friends, often barefoot on dusty fields. Even as a child, Bolt's speed set him apart. His parents, Wellesley and Jennifer Bolt, were hard-working grocery store owners who supported their son's passion for athletics.

Bolt's introduction to competitive sprinting came in primary school, where his natural speed quickly caught the attention of his teachers and coaches. At age 12, he entered his first track meet and won the 100-meter race. His talent was undeniable, but Bolt initially preferred cricket, idolizing stars like Brian Lara. It was his cricket coach who suggested he focus on sprinting, recognizing his potential to excel in track and field.

At age 14, Bolt enrolled at William Knibb Memorial High School, a school known for its strong athletics program. There, he met his first coach, Pablo McNeil, a former Olympic sprinter. McNeil saw incredible potential in Bolt but struggled to channel the teenager's boundless energy and playful nature. Bolt loved to joke around, and his carefree attitude often led to clashes with McNeil, who pushed him to take training seriously.

Despite his occasional lack of focus, Bolt's talent was unstoppable. At age 15, he burst onto the international scene at the 2002 World Junior Championships in Kingston, Jamaica. Competing in front of a home crowd, Bolt won the 200-meter race, becoming the youngest world junior champion in history. The victory made him a national hero overnight, and Jamaica's track and field community knew they had discovered something special.

Over the next few years, Bolt continued to shine, but his journey wasn't without setbacks. As he transitioned from junior to senior competition, injuries began to plague his career. Hamstring problems kept him from performing at his best, and doubts emerged about whether he could handle the pressure of the global stage. Bolt also faced criticism for his relaxed demeanor, which some mistook for a lack of commitment. However, beneath his laid-back exterior was a fierce competitor determined to prove himself.

In 2004, Bolt qualified for his first Olympics in Athens at the age of 17. But his Olympic debut ended in disappointment when a leg injury forced him to withdraw from his first-round heat in the 200 meters. The setback was a blow to his confidence, but Bolt refused to give up. He began working with a new coach, Glen Mills, who would become a transformative figure in his career.

Under Mills' guidance, Bolt matured as an athlete. Mills encouraged Bolt to adopt a more disciplined approach to training while allowing him to maintain his playful personality. The partnership paid off, and Bolt began to unlock his full potential. By 2007, he was competing at the highest level and setting personal bests in both the 100 and 200 meters.

The breakthrough came in 2008. At a meet in New York City, Bolt shattered the world record in the 100 meters, clocking a time of 9.72 seconds. The performance stunned the athletics world and set the stage for his historic run at the Beijing Olympics later that year.

In Beijing, Bolt delivered one of the most dominant performances in Olympic history. In the 100-meter final, he burst out of the blocks and effortlessly pulled away from the field. By the time he crossed the finish line, arms outstretched in celebration, he had set a new world record of 9.69 seconds. What made the feat even more astonishing was that he slowed down in the final meters to celebrate, leaving fans and commentators wondering how much faster he could have gone.

Bolt wasn't done. Days later, he won gold in the 200 meters, breaking another world record with a time of 19.30 seconds. He capped off his Olympic campaign by anchoring Jamaica's 4x100-meter relay team to gold and a third world record. Bolt's triple-gold performance made him a global superstar and the face of athletics.

Over the next decade, Bolt's dominance continued. At the 2009 World Championships in Berlin, he shattered his own records in both the 100 and 200 meters, running 9.58 and 19.19 seconds, respectively. These times remain the fastest ever recorded, cementing Bolt's status as the greatest sprinter in history.

Bolt's success wasn't just about his speed—it was also about his charisma. With his playful pre-race antics, signature "Lightning Bolt" pose, and infectious smile, Bolt endeared himself to fans worldwide. He brought a sense of joy and excitement to the track, making every race a spectacle. Fans loved his humility and his ability to connect with people from all walks of life.

At the 2012 London Olympics, Bolt defended his titles in the 100 and 200 meters and added another gold in the 4x100-meter relay. He repeated the feat at the 2016 Rio Olympics, becoming the first athlete to win gold in the 100, 200, and 4x100 meters at three consecutive Games—a record unlikely to be matched.

Behind the scenes, Bolt remained grounded. Despite his fame, he never forgot his roots, frequently returning to Jamaica to give back to his community. He supported numerous charitable initiatives, including funding scholarships and providing resources for young athletes. Bolt became an ambassador for his country, promoting Jamaican culture and inspiring the next generation.

In 2017, Bolt announced his retirement from track and field. His final race at the World Championships in London ended in heartbreak when he pulled up with an injury during the 4x100-meter relay. Though it wasn't the fairy-tale ending fans had hoped for, it didn't diminish his legacy. Bolt retired as an eight-time Olympic gold medalist, 11-time world champion, and the holder of multiple world records.

Today, Usain Bolt's impact extends far beyond athletics. He is a symbol of what can be achieved through talent, hard work, and an unshakable belief in oneself. His story inspires not just athletes, but anyone striving to reach their full potential.

"Don't think about the start of the race; think about the finish."

— Usain Bolt

The Miracle at Augusta: Tiger Woods' 2019 Masters Comeback

A Champion's Return Against All Odds

On April 14, 2019, the world watched in awe as Tiger Woods stood on the 18th green at Augusta National Golf Club, donning his fifth Masters green jacket. It wasn't just another victory for one of golf's greatest players—it was a testament to resilience, perseverance, and the indomitable spirit of a champion. The journey to that moment had been long and arduous, marked by personal struggles, devastating injuries, and a career many thought was over. But Tiger Woods' 2019 Masters victory wasn't just about golf; it was about redemption.

Tiger Woods was born Eldrick Tont Woods on December 30, 1975, in Cypress, California. From an early age, it was clear he was a prodigy. By the time he was two years old, he was swinging a golf club with uncanny precision, and by the time he was a teenager, he was dominating junior tournaments. His father, Earl Woods, was his mentor and biggest supporter, instilling in him a relentless work ethic and an unshakable belief in his abilities.

Tiger's rise to fame was meteoric. After a stellar amateur career, he turned professional in 1996 at the age of 20. Within a year, he had captured his first major championship, winning the Masters in 1997 by a record 12 strokes. Dressed in his signature Sunday red, Tiger delivered a performance so dominant that it transformed the sport overnight. Golf, once seen as a pastime for older players, suddenly had a charismatic, young superstar who could draw crowds like no one else.

Over the next decade, Tiger dominated the sport like no one before him. By 2008, he had amassed 14 major championship victories, just four shy of Jack Nicklaus' record of 18. His combination of power, precision, and mental toughness made him nearly unbeatable. But behind the trophies and accolades, cracks were beginning to show.

In 2009, Tiger's personal life imploded. A car accident outside his Florida home revealed a series of infidelities, leading to a public scandal and the breakdown of his marriage. The fallout was brutal. Sponsors dropped him, his public image suffered, and his once-invincible aura seemed shattered. On the golf course, Tiger struggled to recapture his form, and injuries began to take a toll.

Between 2014 and 2017, Tiger underwent multiple surgeries, including four on his back. The once-dominant golfer could barely swing a club without pain. At his lowest point, he admitted he wasn't sure if he'd ever play competitively again. In 2017, he was arrested for driving under the influence, a low moment that seemed to signal the end of his career. The man who had once ruled golf was now a shadow of his former self.

But Tiger Woods wasn't finished. Despite the setbacks, he refused to give up. In 2018, after undergoing a spinal fusion surgery that finally alleviated his pain, Tiger began his comeback. Slowly but surely, he started to show flashes of his old brilliance. That September, he won the Tour Championship, his first victory in five years. The win was emotional, but many still doubted whether he could contend for another major championship.

The 2019 Masters presented the ultimate test. Augusta National, with its rolling greens and unforgiving hazards, is one of the most challenging courses in the world. The tournament is steeped in tradition, and the pressure of competing on its storied fairways is unmatched. For Tiger, the Masters was more than a golf tournament—it was the site of his first major victory and a place where he had achieved some of his greatest triumphs.

Tiger entered the tournament ranked 12th in the world, a remarkable achievement considering where he had been just a year earlier. But few believed he could win. Younger players like Brooks Koepka, Rory McIlroy, and Dustin Johnson were dominating the sport, and Tiger's best days seemed behind him. Still, the fans were hopeful. Could this be the tournament where the Tiger of old would reemerge?

The first three days of the Masters were a showcase of Tiger's grit and determination. He played steady, patient golf, staying near the top of the leaderboard without taking unnecessary risks. By the end of Saturday's third round, he was two strokes behind Francesco Molinari, the reigning British Open champion and the tournament leader. It was the closest Tiger had been to winning a major in over a decade.

Sunday, April 14, 2019, was a day for the history books. With the threat of bad weather, tournament officials decided to start the final round earlier than usual. The final group, including Tiger, Molinari, and Tony Finau, teed off in the morning, setting the stage for a dramatic finish.

As the round unfolded, Tiger's experience and composure began to shine. Molinari, who had been rock-solid all week, faltered on the 12th hole, hitting his tee shot into the water and double-bogeying. The mistake opened the door for Tiger, who seized the moment. On the par-3 16th hole, Tiger hit an unforgettable tee shot that rolled within feet of the hole, setting up a crucial birdie. The roars from the crowd echoed through Augusta, a sound that hadn't been heard in years.

By the 18th hole, Tiger had a two-stroke lead. As he walked up the fairway, the crowd erupted in cheers, chanting his name. Fans of all ages, some of whom had grown up watching Tiger, were witnessing history. With nerves of steel, Tiger sank his final putt, securing his fifth Masters title and 15th major championship. The scene on the 18th green was one of pure emotion. Tiger raised his arms in triumph, his face a mix of joy and relief. He hugged his children, who had never seen their father win a major, and shared the moment with his mother and longtime caddie.

Tiger's victory at the 2019 Masters was more than just a comeback—it was a redemption story for the ages. It was a reminder that greatness isn't just about talent; it's about resilience, hard work, and the refusal to give up. For fans around the world, it was a moment of inspiration, proof that even the greatest can stumble but still find a way to rise again.

Today, Tiger Woods' 2019 Masters win stands as one of the most iconic moments in sports history. It is a testament to the power of perseverance and a reminder that no matter how far you fall, it's never too late to reclaim your greatness.

"People don't understand that when I grew up, I was never the most talented. I was never the biggest. I was never the fastest. I was certainly never the strongest. The only thing I had was my work ethic, and that's what has gotten me this far."

— Tiger Woods

Muhammad Ali: The Rumble in the Jungle

How the Greatest Boxer Stunned the World in Zaire

In the heart of Africa, under the sweltering skies of Kinshasa, Zaire (now the Democratic Republic of Congo), one of the most legendary moments in sports history unfolded. On October 30, 1974, Muhammad Ali faced

George Foreman in a fight that was more than just a boxing match—it was a battle of wills, a clash of personalities, and a symbol of resilience and hope for millions around the world. Dubbed "The Rumble in the Jungle," this fight would cement Ali's legacy not only as a boxer but as one of the greatest icons of all time.

Muhammad Ali was born Cassius Marcellus Clay Jr. on January 17, 1942, in Louisville, Kentucky. From a young age, he showed a passion for competition and an innate charisma that set him apart. Ali's journey to greatness began when, at 12 years old, he took up boxing after his bicycle was stolen. Determined to fight whoever had taken it, Ali instead found himself in the gym, learning how to channel his anger and energy into the art of boxing. Under the guidance of coach Joe Martin, Ali quickly rose through the amateur ranks, showcasing his natural speed, agility, and determination.

At 18, Ali won a gold medal in boxing at the 1960 Rome Olympics, capturing the attention of the world with his dazzling style and unshakable confidence. Turning professional soon after, he became known not just for his skill in the ring but for his larger-than-life personality. Ali's ability to "float like a butterfly, sting like a bee" earned him the heavyweight title in 1964 when he defeated Sonny Liston in a stunning upset.

But Ali was more than just an athlete; he was a cultural icon. He changed his name after converting to Islam and refused to fight in the Vietnam War, a decision that cost him his boxing license and his heavyweight title. For three years, Ali was barred from competing, but he never wavered in his convictions. When he returned to the ring in 1970, he was determined to reclaim his place at the top.

By 1974, Ali had faced setbacks, including two losses—one to Joe Frazier and another to Ken Norton—that led many to believe his best days were behind him. Meanwhile, George Foreman was the reigning heavyweight champion, an undefeated powerhouse who had demolished both Frazier and Norton in dominant fashion. Foreman's strength and knockout power made him seem invincible, and many doubted Ali could stand a chance against him.

The fight was set to take place in Kinshasa, Zaire, and was promoted by Don King, a flamboyant figure who promised a $10 million purse to be split between the fighters. The location itself added a sense of grandeur and importance to the event. For Ali, fighting in Africa held deep meaning. He embraced his African heritage and saw the bout as an opportunity to connect with his roots and inspire people across the continent.

The buildup to the fight was electric. Ali's charisma was on full display as he won over the local crowd with his charm and wit. Chanting "Ali, bomaye!"—which means "Ali, kill him!" in Lingala—the people of Kinshasa made it clear who their favorite was. Ali fed off their energy, turning every press conference and public appearance into a performance. Foreman, on the other hand, was quiet and reserved, his imposing demeanor adding to his mystique.

As the fight approached, Ali devised a strategy that would shock the world. Known for his speed and footwork, Ali was expected to use his agility to dance around the ring and avoid Foreman's devastating punches. But Ali and his trainer, Angelo Dundee, knew they needed something unconventional to counter Foreman's power. They developed a plan Ali called the "rope-a-dope."

The strategy was simple but risky. Instead of avoiding Foreman's punches, Ali would lean against the ropes, covering up and letting Foreman expend his energy by throwing heavy shots. The idea was to tire Foreman out, then attack when he was vulnerable. It was a gamble, but Ali was confident it would work.

On fight night, the atmosphere in the stadium was electric. Under the lights of the open-air arena, with millions watching around the world, Ali and Foreman stepped into the ring. From the opening bell, Ali's plan became clear. He leaned against the ropes, absorbing Foreman's punches and taunting him with remarks like, "Is that all you got, George?" While the strategy confused spectators and commentators, it infuriated Foreman, who continued to throw punch after punch.

Round after round, Ali executed the rope-a-dope perfectly. Foreman, known for his brute strength, began to slow down, his punches losing their power. Meanwhile, Ali occasionally unleashed flurries of punches to keep Foreman off balance, showcasing his speed and precision. The crowd, initially uncertain about Ali's tactics, began to see the genius of his plan.

By the eighth round, Foreman was visibly exhausted. Ali, sensing his moment, unleashed a quick combination that sent Foreman to the canvas. The champion tried to get up, but the referee counted him out. Ali had done the impossible. Against all odds, he defeated the seemingly invincible George Foreman to reclaim the heavyweight title.

The crowd erupted in celebration as Ali raised his arms in triumph. In one of the most iconic moments in sports history, Ali stood atop the ropes, shouting to the world that he was the greatest. The victory wasn't just about boxing—it was a triumph of strategy, resilience, and belief in oneself. Ali had proven that intelligence and heart could overcome brute strength.

The Rumble in the Jungle solidified Ali's place as a legend, not just in boxing but in global culture. His ability to overcome adversity, both inside and outside the ring, inspired millions and made him a symbol of hope and determination. For the people of Zaire, the fight was a moment of pride and unity, a celebration of their heritage and the spirit of perseverance.

Today, Muhammad Ali's legacy lives on as a testament to the power of courage, conviction, and the will to defy expectations. The Rumble in the Jungle remains one of the greatest stories in sports history, a reminder that greatness isn't just about winning—it's about inspiring others to believe in the impossible.

"Impossible is nothing."
— **Muhammad Ali**

Michael Phelps: The Greatest Olympian of All Time

How an Unstoppable Swimmer Made History in the Pool

Michael Phelps is a name synonymous with greatness. As the most decorated Olympian in history, Phelps didn't just set records—he shattered them, achieving feats that seemed almost superhuman. Over five Olympic Games, Phelps won an astonishing 28 medals, 23 of them gold. But his journey to becoming the "Greatest Olympian of All Time" wasn't just about his victories in the pool. It was a story of perseverance, dedication, and overcoming personal struggles to achieve the extraordinary.

Michael Fred Phelps II was born on June 30, 1985, in Baltimore, Maryland. From an early age, Michael was energetic and competitive, traits that made him a natural athlete. However, his childhood was also filled with challenges. At age nine, Phelps was diagnosed with Attention Deficit Hyperactivity Disorder (ADHD), which made it difficult for him to focus in school. His mother, Debbie, a middle school principal, sought ways to channel Michael's boundless energy into something positive. Swimming became the answer.

Phelps first entered the water at the age of seven, following in the footsteps of his older sisters, Whitney and Hilary, who were both swimmers. While he initially disliked putting his face in the water, his coaches quickly recognized his potential. With his tall, lanky frame, large hands, and size 14 feet, Phelps had the perfect build for swimming. Under the guidance of his coach, Bob Bowman, Phelps began training rigorously. Bowman saw in Phelps a rare combination of physical talent and mental toughness, and their partnership would become one of the most successful in sports history.

By the time he was 15, Phelps was already making waves on the international stage. In 2000, he qualified for the Sydney Olympics, becoming the youngest male swimmer to compete for Team USA in 68 years. Though he didn't medal, the experience fueled his determination. Just a year later, Phelps broke his first world record in the 200-meter butterfly, becoming the youngest male swimmer ever to achieve such a feat. It was clear that the young swimmer was destined for greatness.

The 2004 Athens Olympics marked Phelps' arrival as a global star. At just 19 years old, he won six gold medals and two bronze, showcasing his versatility by competing in a range of events, from sprints to long-distance races. His performance drew comparisons to Mark Spitz, the legendary swimmer who had won seven golds in a single Olympics in 1972. For Phelps, the comparison was more than flattery—it was a goal. He set his sights on surpassing Spitz's record, an ambition that would define the next phase of his career.

Leading up to the 2008 Beijing Olympics, Phelps trained with an intensity that bordered on obsession. He swam six hours a day, six days a week, covering an average of 80,000 meters per week. His diet was equally extreme; Phelps consumed around 12,000 calories a day to fuel his grueling workouts. The discipline paid off. In Beijing, Phelps delivered what many consider the greatest single performance in Olympic history.

Over the course of nine days, Phelps competed in eight events—and won gold in all of them. Each race seemed more dramatic than the last. In the 100-meter butterfly, Phelps won by just one one-hundredth of a second, out-touching his opponent in a finish so close it had to be reviewed multiple times. In the 4x100-meter freestyle relay, Team USA staged a stunning comeback, with anchor Jason Lezak swimming the fastest split in history to secure the gold. With each victory, Phelps edged closer to history. When he won his eighth gold medal, breaking Spitz's record, he became a global phenomenon. His triumph wasn't just about the medals; it was about his ability to thrive under immense pressure and deliver in the most challenging moments.

Despite his success, Phelps' journey wasn't without struggles. After the 2008 Olympics, he experienced a period of aimlessness and exhaustion. The intense pressure to succeed, coupled with the physical demands of training, took a toll on his mental health. In 2012, after winning four golds and two silvers at the London Olympics, Phelps announced his retirement. But retirement proved difficult. Struggling with depression and searching for purpose, Phelps found himself in a dark place.

In 2014, Phelps was arrested for driving under the influence, a turning point that forced him to confront his inner demons. With the support of his family and friends, Phelps sought help, entering a rehabilitation program and beginning a journey of self-discovery. He also reconnected with his love for swimming, deciding to return to the sport not for records, but for the joy it brought him.

Phelps' comeback culminated in the 2016 Rio Olympics, where he competed in his fifth and final Games. At 31, he was no longer the unstoppable force of his youth, but his experience and determination carried him to five gold medals and one silver. The most memorable moment came in the 200-meter butterfly, a race Phelps had lost in London. In Rio, he reclaimed the gold, showing the world that even the greatest can rise again after setbacks.

When Phelps retired for good after Rio, his tally of 28 Olympic medals—23 of them gold—was a record unlikely to be broken. But his legacy extends far beyond the numbers. Phelps revolutionized swimming with his versatility, work ethic, and ability to perform under pressure. He also used his platform to advocate for mental health, speaking openly about his struggles and encouraging others to seek help.

Today, Michael Phelps remains an inspiration to athletes and fans around the world. His story is a reminder that greatness isn't just about talent—it's about resilience, self-belief, and the courage to overcome challenges. The boy who once disliked putting his face in the water became the greatest swimmer in history, proving that with dedication and heart, anything is possible.

"You can't put a limit on anything. The more you dream, the farther you get."

— Michael Phelps

The Legacy of Champions

As you've read through these incredible stories, you've seen that sports are about much more than winning trophies or breaking records. They're about the human spirit—about courage, perseverance, and the willingness to chase dreams, no matter how difficult the journey. Each story in this book has shown us that greatness isn't just measured by achievements but by the heart and determination it takes to achieve them.

From Muhammad Ali's unwavering confidence to Simone Biles' strength in overcoming adversity, and from Tiger Woods' remarkable comeback to Usain Bolt's electrifying speed, these athletes have inspired generations. They remind us that no matter where we come from or what obstacles we face, we have the power to rise, push forward, and make our dreams a reality.

This book isn't just about their stories; it's about the inspiration you can take from them. Whether it's on the field, in the classroom, or in everyday life, the lessons these champions teach us are universal: Work hard. Stay focused. Believe in yourself. Never give up.

As you close this book, remember that the next great story could be yours. Whatever challenges or goals you face, approach them with the same determination and heart as these extraordinary athletes. The legacy of champions is not just in what they achieve but in how they inspire others to believe in the impossible.

Now it's your turn to chase greatness. What will your story be?

Made in United States
Orlando, FL
10 March 2025